RAND | NATIONAL DEFENSE RESEARCH INSTITUTE

Homeland Security National Risk Characterization

Risk Assessment Methodology

Henry H. Willis, Mary Tighe, Andrew Lauland, Liisa Ecola,
Shoshana R. Shelton, Meagan L. Smith, John G. Rivers,
Kristin J. Leuschner, Terry Marsh, Daniel M. Gerstein

Prepared for the Department of Homeland Security Office of Policy

Approved for public release; distribution unlimited

For more information on this publication, visit **www.rand.org/t/RR2140**

Library of Congress Cataloging-in-Publication Data
ISBN: 978-0-8330-9968-6

Published by the RAND Corporation, Santa Monica, Calif.
© Copyright 2018 RAND Corporation
RAND® is a registered trademark.

Cover: Getty Images/tonefotografia.

Limited Print and Electronic Distribution Rights

This document and trademark(s) contained herein are protected by law. This representation of RAND intellectual property is provided for noncommercial use only. Unauthorized posting of this publication online is prohibited. Permission is given to duplicate this document for personal use only, as long as it is unaltered and complete. Permission is required from RAND to reproduce, or reuse in another form, any of its research documents for commercial use. For information on reprint and linking permissions, please visit www.rand.org/pubs/permissions.

The RAND Corporation is a research organization that develops solutions to public policy challenges to help make communities throughout the world safer and more secure, healthier and more prosperous. RAND is nonprofit, nonpartisan, and committed to the public interest.

RAND's publications do not necessarily reflect the opinions of its research clients and sponsors.

Support RAND
Make a tax-deductible charitable contribution at
www.rand.org/giving/contribute

www.rand.org

Preface

In 2016, the U.S. Department of Homeland Security (DHS), Office of Policy—Strategy, Plans, Analysis, and Risk (SPAR), asked the RAND National Defense Research Institute to design and implement a risk identification and characterization of natural and manmade threats and hazards to identify the greatest risks to homeland security and support prioritization of DHS mission elements as part of DHS strategic planning processes.

This report describes the risk assessment methodology RAND researchers developed to address these goals. It also presents summary sheets of threats and hazards to inform discussion of DHS risk management priorities, which are included in an accompanying For Official Use Only volume. A separate policy-oriented report will be issued by the DHS Office of Policy to present key findings about the risks from homeland security threats and hazards and the priorities for managing them.

This research was sponsored by SPAR and conducted within the RAND Homeland Security and Defense Center, a joint center of RAND Justice, Infrastructure, and Environment and the RAND National Defense Research Institute (NDRI), a federally funded research and development center sponsored by the Office of the Secretary of Defense, the Joint Staff, the Unified Combatant Commands, the Navy, the Marine Corps, the defense agencies, and the defense Intelligence Community.

Comments or questions on this draft report should be addressed to the project leader Henry Willis at hwillis@rand.org.

For more information on NDRI, see www.rand.org/nsrd.

Contents

Figures and Tables

Figures

Tables

Summary

In 2016, the U.S. Department of Homeland Security (DHS), Office of Policy—Strategy, Plans, Analysis, and Risk (SPAR), asked the RAND National Defense Research Institute (NDRI) to design and implement a homeland security national risk assessment to help inform DHS strategic planning by identifying and characterizing natural hazards and threats to the nation. This assessment can be used by DHS to assist in identifying the greatest risks to homeland security and to support prioritization of DHS mission elements.

This report responds to SPAR's request. It describes the risk assessment methodology developed by the RAND Corporation and presents summary sheets of threats and hazards intended to inform discussion of DHS risk management priorities. The methodology is also designed to address important critiques made by the U.S. Government Accountability Office (GAO) in its assessments of the 2010 and 2014 Quadrennial Homeland Security Reviews (QHSRs).

To address the GAO critiques, the approach described in this report describes a set of threats and hazards that is *strategically relevant* and does so *in a consistent way.* Furthermore, the process for selecting and characterizing the hazards uses a *methodology that is repeatable and transparent.*

Steps in the Risk Assessment Methodology

To inform the discussion of the national security environment in prior QHSRs, SPAR developed a Homeland Security National Risk Characterization (HSNRC), first issued in 2014, which examined key threats, hazards, and other factors that pose a substantial risk to homeland security or that could significantly affect DHS's pursuit of its stated missions and goals. The risk assessment methodology described in this report is intended to support DHS in developing the 2018 HSNRC.

The steps in the risk assessment methodology to support the HSNRC are shown in Figure S.1. This methodology involves four main steps, as well as an ongoing process of stakeholder engagement, which is described first.

Figure S.1
Framework for the Risk Assessment Methodology to Inform the
Homeland Security National Risk Characterization

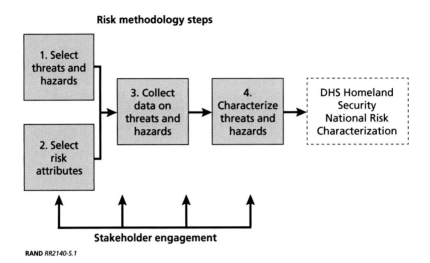

RAND RR2140-S.1

Key Supporting Activity: Stakeholder Engagement

A key activity running through the entirety of the risk assessment methodology is stake-holder engagement with DHS headquarters and components through the DHS Risk Executive Steering Committee (Risk ESC) and the Committee's Technical Working Group (TWG). Early and consistent stakeholder engagement is intended to (1) ensure that the scope of the HSNRC reflects the priorities of DHS, its office, and its compo-nents; and (2) provide opportunity for review and comment on the development of the methodology and the use of data to inform the analysis.

Step 1. Select Threats and Hazards

The first step in the risk assessment methodology is to determine which threats and hazards to include in the HSNRC. This step has three parts: generating a list of threats and hazards to be considered, selecting screening criteria, and using the criteria to select a prioritized set of hazards.

Part 1: Generate a List of Threats and Hazards

The first part is to generate an initial list of hazards for consideration. The develop-ment of this list should be guided by DHS's strategic perspective, informed by prior risk analyses, and selected through deliberation among DHS components and offices.

Part 2: Select Screening Criteria

The second part is to screen hazards based on the following screening criteria guided by the purpose of strategic planning effort and reviewed with the Risk ESC:

- Is the threat or hazard exogenous to the homeland security enterprise?[1]
- Is the threat or hazard the result of either discrete events or persistent phenomena, not events that affect threats and hazards (e.g., climate change, which could change exposures to flooding and hurricanes) or are the effects of hazard (e.g., loss of a fishery)?
- Is the threat or hazard related to DHS strategic priorities as identified in department-level strategy and planning documents, particularly the prior QHSR?
- Is DHS charged with mitigating the risks from the threat or hazard, in either a lead or major supporting role?
- Does the threat or hazard have the potential for significant impact on at least one of the following: (1) health, safety, and security; (2) the economy; (3) the natural environment; and (4) governance?

Part 3: Select a Prioritized Set of Threats and Hazards

The third part of the threat and hazard identification step is to use the screening criteria to select a prioritized set of hazards and threats for consideration. The final approved list of threats and hazards is shown in Table S.1.

Step 2. Select Risk Attributes

After the threat and hazard identification step is under way, the next step in the risk assessment methodology is to select the attributes used to describe threats and hazards, that is, the characterization of the way threats or hazards affect the nation. This step involves two parts. The first is determination of a set of broad criteria for risk attributes, and the second is applying the criteria to select the attributes.

Part 1: Select Criteria for Risk Attributes

Risk attributes should be selected using the following screening approach. This approach was designed to reflect the range of potential effects by focusing on four types of operationally relevant impacts: (1) health, safety, and security; (2) economic; (3) environmental; and (4) governance. To ensure they are useful within the HSNRC, each attribute should also be

- *measurable*, meaning that attributes are conceptually clear enough so that measures can be defined to describe the nature and extent of impacts
- *operationally relevant*, meaning that information to describe threats and hazards is available within the time and resource constraints of the HSNRC.

Furthermore, attributes should describe the uncertainty about threats and hazards.

---

[1]   The HSNRC did not include threats or hazards that are a result of the enterprise's structure, budgets, and oversight, each of which would be relevant to an enterprise risk assessment.

Table S.1
Final List of Threats and Hazards Approved for
Inclusion in the Homeland Security National Risk
Characterization

Terrorist Threats

- Attack on leadership
- Attacks targeting critical infrastructure
- Biological weapon attack
- Chemical weapon attack
- Nuclear attack
- Radiological attack
- Small arms/explosive attack on populations

Cyber Threats

- Cyber attack on critical infrastructure networks
- Cyber attack that steals sensitive government data
- Cyber attack on government networks

Illegal Activities

- Counterfeit goods
- Human trafficking
- Illegal migration
- Mass migration
- Transnational drug trafficking

Natural Hazards

- Drought
- Earthquake
- Flooding
- Hurricane
- Space weather
- Tsunami
- Volcano
- Wildfire

Health Hazards

- Agricultural plant disease outbreak
- Foreign animal disease outbreak
- Transnational communicable disease

Infrastructure Hazards

- Technical failure or industrial accident of critical infrastructure caused by human error or age

Other

- Electromagnetic pulse

The set of attributes as a whole should also balance three criteria: completeness, uniqueness, and conciseness. *Completeness* is needed to ensure that the full range of attributes is considered in setting priorities for risk management. *Uniqueness* is important to ensure that each attribute reflects a distinctive dimension of risk, that is, to avoid "double counting" of risk impacts. *Conciseness* helps facilitate analysis, thus ensuring that the information in the risk assessments can be used to support decisionmaking. The number of attributes should be as few as possible, since it is often easier to make comparisons or decisions when fewer dimensions are analyzed.

Part 2: Select Attributes

The criteria described in Part 1 are used to select risk attributes. In selecting attributes for the HSNRC, we first examined completed comparative risk assessments to identify possible attributes that might be used to describe threats and hazards in the HSNRC. Then, starting from the list of possible attributes, we identified a set of the smallest number of attributes that would also meet the criteria of completeness, uniqueness, and conciseness while representing the dimensions addressed in prior risk assessments.

Tables S.2 and S.3 show the final set of attributes for describing risk in the HSNRC. Table S.2 focuses on consequences (health, safety, security; economic; environmental; governance), while Table S.3 focuses on uncertainty. Risk assessments will

Table S.2
Final Set of Attributes of Consequences for Describing Risk in the Homeland Security National Risk Characterization

Impact Category	Attribute	Units
Health, Safety, and Security	Deaths	Number of deaths, described as average per year and greatest number in a single episode
	Injuries and illnesses	Number of injuries and illnesses, described as average per year and greatest number in a single episode
	National well-being Loss of confidence in societal and personal health, safety, and/or security	Qualitative assessment of the expected impact on perceptions that government can provide desired security, described as average annual impact and greatest impact in a single episode (low, medium, high)
Economic	Economic damages	Dollars, described as average annual impact and greatest impact in a single episode
	Greatest critical or lifeline infrastructure effects from a single episode	Qualitative constructed scale reflecting duration and number of affected customers (low, medium, high)
Environmental	Greatest environmental damage in a single episode	Qualitative constructed scale accounting for effects on species, ecosystems, and viewscapes that reflects time required for remediation and geographic extent of damage (low, medium, high)
Governance	Greatest disruption of National Essential Functions in a single episode	Qualitative constructed scale accounting for the population affected and duration of disruptions (low, medium, high)

Table S.3
Final Set of Attributes of Uncertainty for Describing Risk in the Homeland Security National Risk Characterization

Attribute	Units
Frequency of occurrence	Description of frequency ranging from daily to millennially
Predictability	Constructed, qualitative scale reflecting the amount of warning for a single episode and the ability to estimate annual impacts (low, medium, high)
Precision	Qualitative aggregated assessment of precision in estimates across all attributes

reflect uncertainty in two ways. First, for each of the attributes using a quantitative measure, descriptions include low, best, and high estimates for that attribute. Second, the attributes in Table S.3—frequency, predictability, and precision—are used to describe other dimensions of the uncertainty surrounding threats and hazards, since these characteristics also influence risk perceptions and decisions about risk management.

Step 3. Collect Data on Threats and Hazards

The third step in the risk assessment process is to collect and analyze government-provided data to describe and characterize the threats and hazards identified in the first step, using the attributes identified in the second step. This approach includes an initial data search conducted by the team, a data call to DHS components, supplementary efforts to address data gaps, and development of the risk summary sheet template to use in writing the risk characterization for each threat/hazard.

We encountered several challenges in the data collection process. In many cases, the materials initially provided did not cover all or map exactly to the selected threats and hazards. The amount and quality of data also varied across threats and hazards. We reported on the data gaps to the TWG and ESC and asked for additional help in addressing the gaps, which the DHS Office of Policy facilitated. While this process was able to address some gaps, in many cases there were gaps that could not be entirely addressed.

Step 4. Characterize Threats and Hazards

The inputs from the first three steps are used to characterize the threats and hazards and produce vetted risk summary sheets to inform discussion of risk management priorities. The risk summary sheets, which are included in a separate For Official Use Only volume, each describe

- the scope of the threat or hazard
- the mechanisms though which the threat or hazard affect the nation
- an overview of the impacts from the threat and hazard to the nation

- the uncertainty surrounding the likelihood and impacts associated with the threat or hazard.

The goal of the risk summary sheets is to provide, in a consistent manner, DHS and its partners across the homeland security enterprise with an overview of how each threat and hazard affects the nation. This overview can serve as a common foundation for analysis of homeland security risks to the nation and priorities for managing them.

However, we note that developing the risk summary sheets involves considerable subjective input. An important part of developing the risk summary sheets, and therefore also of the HSNRC methodology, involves deciding *how* to describe the impacts of threats and hazards. Each risk summary sheet must consider how prior assessments were interpreted when making assessments for each attribute and provide citations for the assessments used. To make assessments for quantitative attributes, summary sheet authors must translate reviewed literature into order-of-magnitude assessments. To make assessments for qualitative attributes, authors must use reviewed literature to make an assessment of each threat and hazard, place it within a defined category of impact, and then translate these defined categories into units of low, medium, or high. The reasoning behind these judgments is documented in the risk summary sheets.

Given the diversity of threats and hazards described, the persistent data gaps, and the many issues that remained open to interpretation, the process of characterizing the threats and hazards in the risk summary sheets required ongoing tradeoffs between (1) the need to maintain consistency and transparency when applying the risk assessment methodology, and (2) the need to exercise judgment in characterizing specific risks.

Risk summary sheets were subjected to review by experts within DHS and at RAND to assess whether the risk assessment approach was applied consistently, data sources used were appropriate, and the impact assessments were consistent with supporting information.

Conclusion

The results of the HSNRC presented in this report were motivated by three goals. First, DHS required a transparent and repeatable process for assessing and comparing strategically significant threats and hazards from which DHS is responsible for protecting the nation. Second, risk assessments produced using the HSNRC process are intended to serve as a common reference point for discussions about how these threats and hazards affect the nation. Third, with a common understanding of the impacts of threats and hazards on the nation, DHS leadership would be enabled to develop and implement strategic plans that direct the department's resources to achieve the desired approach to protecting the nation from threats, responding to disasters, and promoting economic resilience.

The HSNRC does not provide all information required to complete this strategic planning process. Steps required to provide additional perspectives that would be required to build from risk assessment to risk management include the following:

- Understand which threats and hazards pose the greatest risk to the nation.
- Identify threats and hazards for which current efforts are disproportionate to risk.
- Provide recommendations on how to further reduce risk.
- Place DHS's role and responsibilities within the larger context of whole-of-government responsibilities for managing the risks from the identified threats and hazards.

Other supporting analyses of the strategic planning process provide this information. By combining the results of the HSNRC with these complementary analyses of DHS authorities, programming, capabilities, and gaps, DHS will be able, if desired, to sort the homeland security risk landscape into problems that are understood well enough and problems that need to be better understood. Similarly, it would be possible to sort the risk landscape into problems for which more can be done and those for which enough is already being done. With insights like these, the department could build the foundation for DHS strategic planning and resource guidance.

Acknowledgments

This work benefited from the assistance and inspiration from numerous colleagues. The authors would particularly like to thank Stuart Evenhaugen, Brian Jackson, Seth Jones, Terrence Kelly, Michael Mazarr, Michael Wetzl, members of the DHS Risk Executive Steering Committee, and members of the Technical Working Group of the Risk Executive Steering Committee. We also thank our RAND colleagues who conducted the peer review of the report and associated risk summary sheets: Jim Bonomo, Colin Clarke, John Davis, Debra Knopman, Chris Schnaubelt, and Melinda Moore. Without the entirety of these contributions, this work would not have been possible.

Abbreviations

DHS	U.S. Department of Homeland Security
ESC	Executive Steering Committee
FEMA	Federal Emergency Management Agency
FY	fiscal year
GAO	U.S. Government Accountability Office
HSNRC	Homeland Security National Risk Characterization
QHSR	Quadrennial Homeland Security Review
SNRA	Strategic National Risk Assessment
SPAR	U.S. Department of Homeland Security, Office of Policy—Strategy, Plans, Analysis, and Risk
TWG	Technical Working Group

CHAPTER ONE

Introduction

In 2016, the U.S. Department of Homeland Security (DHS), Office of Policy—Strategy, Plans, Analysis, and Risk (SPAR), asked the RAND National Defense Research Institute to design and implement a homeland security national risk assessment that would inform DHS strategic planning by identifying and characterizing natural hazards and threats to the nation. The assessment can be used by DHS to assist in identifying the greatest risks to homeland security and to support prioritization of DHS mission elements.

The purpose of this report is to describe the risk assessment methodology developed by the RAND team and present summary sheets of threats and hazards (included in a separate For Official Use Only volume) to inform discussion of DHS risk management priorities. A separate report issued by the DHS Office of Policy (DHS Policy) will present key findings about the risks from homeland security threats and hazards along with priorities for managing them.

The remainder of this introduction provides background on the development of the risk assessment methodology and an overview of the steps in that methodology.

Background

The vision of DHS is to ensure a homeland that is "safe, secure, and resilient against terrorism and other hazards, where American interests, aspirations, and way of life can thrive" (DHS, 2017). The 2014 Quadrennial Homeland Security Review (QHSR) defined the department's five core homeland security missions as (1) prevent terrorism and enhance security, (2) secure and manage U.S. borders, (3) enforce and administer U.S. immigration laws, (4) safeguard and secure cyberspace, and (5) ensure resilience to disasters as well as the overarching mission of maturing the homeland security enterprise (DHS, 2014b).

Within DHS, SPAR is responsible for developing analytically based, technically defensible, high-impact products that improve the strategic direction, integration, and decisionmaking of DHS and the homeland security enterprise. Its responsibilities include leading the development of DHS strategic planning and ensuring that DHS strategy, planning, and analysis have the intended beneficial impact on homeland security activities, including the strategic management of those missions prioritized in the strategic planning guidance.

The Quadrennial Homeland Security Review

Since fiscal year (FY) 2009, DHS has been required by Congress to conduct a QHSR every four years to provide "a comprehensive examination of the homeland security strategy of the Nation, including recommendations regarding the long-term strategy and priorities of the Nation for homeland security and guidance on the programs, assets, capabilities, budget, policies, and authorities of the Department" (DHS, 2014b, p. 11).[1] The QHSR is intended to address threats to national security and presents a framework for the nation's strategic response. The strategy laid out in the QHSR is not limited to DHS, but focuses on the homeland security enterprise as a whole, including federal, state, local, tribal, and territorial governments; nongovernmental organizations; the private sector; and individuals, families, and communities (DHS, 2010, p. v).

DHS has conducted two QHSRs to date, published in 2010 and 2014. The 2010 QHSR focused on answering the question "What is homeland security?"—laying out (1) the vision for homeland security, (2) the five mission areas described above, and (3) goals and objectives for each mission area (DHS, 2010). The 2014 QHSR continued to adhere to the five homeland security missions described in the 2010 QHSR while also seeking to reflect the ways in which the nation's homeland security architecture had matured over the previous four years. The 2014 QHSR set forth "risk-informed strategic priorities" that addressed the mission areas and were used to drive operational planning; it also included analysis of resource and capability options (DHS, 2014b, p. 33).

Both the 2010 and 2014 QHSRs linked the homeland security agenda to existing national security concerns, such as threats and hazards that challenge U.S. interests from a homeland security perspective. As explained in the 2014 QHSR, a key purpose of the quadrennial review is "to identify and describe the threats to the Nation's homeland security interests" (DHS, 2014b, pp. 17–18). This examination of threats and hazards is used to characterize homeland security missions, identify strategic challenges, and develop strategic priorities.

To inform the discussion of the national security environment in DHS strategic planning, SPAR developed a Homeland Security National Risk Characterization (HSNRC), first issued in 2014, which examined key threats, hazards, and other factors that pose a substantial risk to homeland security or that could significantly affect DHS's pursuit of its stated missions and goals (DHS, 2014a). The risk assessment

---

[1]   The legal requirement for the QHSR and report is found in Section 707 of the Homeland Security Act of 2002 (P.L. 107-296), as amended by the Implementing Recommendations of the 9/11 Commission Act of 2007 (P.L. 110-53).

methodology described in this report is intended to support DHS in developing the 2018 HSNRC as part of the ongoing strategic planning process.

U.S. Government Accountability Office Assessment of the 2010 and 2014 QHSRs

The risk assessment methodology described in this report is also designed to address important critiques made by the U.S. Government Accountability Office (GAO) in its assessments of the 2010 and 2014 QHSRs. For both reports, GAO examined the strategic frameworks used in identifying and characterizing risks and hazards, the extent and timing of stakeholder engagement efforts, and the extent to which congressional reporting requirements were addressed. Findings from both assessments were summarized in a March 2016 report to Congress (GAO, 2016). Two areas of GAO's critiques are particularly relevant to the development of the risk assessment methodology.

First, GAO identified issues with DHS's process for assessing threats and hazards. Regarding the 2010 QHSR, GAO noted that DHS "did not use risk information to inform QHSR implementation" (p. 2). In 2014, SPAR developed the HSNRC in part to address this issue. While GAO subsequently acknowledged that DHS took some steps to use risk information to inform the 2014 QHSR, its assessment of the 2014 QHSR found that the QHSR did not provide sufficient documentation of the methods used to identify threats, vulnerabilities, and risks. This gap limited the "reproducibility and defensibility" of the results (GAO, 2016, p. 20). The report noted: "Without sufficient documentation, the QHSR risk results cannot easily be validated or the assumptions tested, hindering DHS's ability to improve future assessments" (GAO, 2016, Highlights). GAO recommended that DHS improve its risk assessment documentation for future QHSRs (GAO, 2016, p. 41).

A second area of GAO's critique relevant to risk assessment methodology concerns the level and type of stakeholder engagement in DHS's process for developing the QHSR. GAO's review of the 2010 QHSR stated that stakeholder engagement could be improved. It emphasized the importance of incorporating early and consistent engagement among DHS leadership, components, and the headquarters office, and recommended that DHS "provide sufficient time for stakeholder consultations and examine how risk information could be used to prioritize mission efforts" (GAO, 2016, p. 2).

Developing an Analytic Framework that Provides Transparency into DHS Strategic Planning and Decisionmaking Process

To address the GAO critiques and related issues identified through DHS's own 2012 HSNRC after-action report (DHS, 2012), DHS sought to develop an analytic framework that provides transparency into DHS's decisionmaking process. The HSNRC is an important component in the development of this process.

The analytic framework used to conduct this HSNRC is guided by three criteria.

First, the HSNRC must describe a set of threats and hazards that is *strategically relevant*. For the purpose of the HSNRC, *threats* are defined as events that result from an individual or group with both the intent and capability to cause harm. Threats include terrorism and illegal activities. In contrast to threats, *hazards* refers to naturally occurring events that lead to harm.

The set of threats and hazards should be related to DHS strategic priorities and to existing and emerging threats and hazards in the time period covered in the period FY 2018–2021. Each threat or hazard in the set must have the potential for significant impact on health, safety, and security; the economy; the natural environment; or governance. Finally, selected threats and hazards must be those for which DHS has the potential to make a significant contribution to further reducing risk.

Second, the HSNRC must describe threats and hazards *in a consistent way*. The approach should draw on current knowledge about the hazard. The description of threats and hazards should describe all aspects (i.e., attributes) of the threats and hazards that affect public concerns, including the nature and extent of uncertainty about the hazard.

Third, the risk assessment process for selecting and characterizing the hazards must use a *methodology that is repeatable and transparent*. These characteristics help to ensure that (1) others will be able to repeat this assessment in the future after reading this report and (2) the assessment would produce similar results if conducted within the context of the same policy priorities, organizational structure, and department authorities.

The risk assessment methodology described in this report is intended to address these three issues in support of the HSNRC.

Overview of Risk Assessment Methodology

To assist SPAR, the RAND team developed a risk assessment methodology and, using this methodology, identified and characterized risks from manmade threats and natural hazards. In developing the risk assessment methodology, we incorporated existing government risk assessment methodologies from the 2014 QHSR's HSNRC, as well as feedback from the 2012 HSNRC after-action report, the 2016 GAO review of the 2014 QHSR, and other documents (DHS, 2012; DHS, 2014a; DHS, 2014b; GAO, 2016).

The methodology standardizes and documents an approach for selecting threats and hazards to be analyzed, describing the impacts and uncertainty of these threats and hazards, and documenting the data used. The development of a repeatable and transparent approach for risk assessment will ensure that the results of the HSNRC are informed by a *deliberative analytic process*. The steps in the risk assessment methodology are described in more detail later in this introduction and in the subsequent chapters of this report.

The risk assessment methodology was developed with continuous stakeholder engagement. To support this effort, both a DHS Risk Executive Steering Committee

(Risk ESC) and a Technical Working Group (TWG) were formed. These committees were established by DHS Policy, and participation was open to all DHS operating components and headquarters offices.

Note that the methodology described in this report is part of a broader analytic framework to support DHS strategic analysis, which also includes steps to integrate results from the HSNRC with results of the DHS Enterprise Report. The DHS Enterprise Report provides a snapshot of the state of DHS programming, budgeting, and capabilities as mapped to threats and hazards being managed. DHS strategic planning will subsequently inform the development of DHS's Future Years Homeland Security Program by identifying opportunities to address mitigable risk for select threats and hazards. Strategic planning will also provide strategic-level observations to inform DHS guidance documents and identify topics and issues for the department's analytic agenda over the next five years.

Steps in the Methodology

The steps in the risk assessment methodology to support the HSNRC are shown in Figure 1.1. This approach is adapted from the Deliberative Method for Ranking Risks, which was originally developed to inform health and safety risk management and was subsequently adapted to inform environmental, environmental health, and homeland security risk management (Florig et al., 2001; Morgan et al., 2001; Willis et al., 2004; Willis et al., 2010; Lundberg and Willis, 2015; Lundberg and Willis, 2016).

The Deliberative Method for Ranking Risks was motivated by observations that, for the purpose of prioritizing risks from threats and hazards, the stated pri-

Figure 1.1
Framework for the Risk Assessment Methodology to Inform the Homeland Security National Risk Characterization

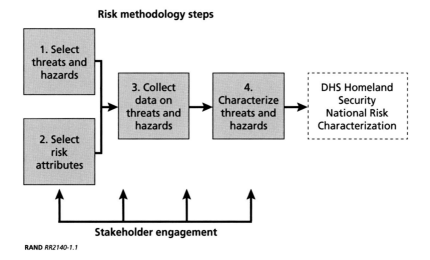

RAND RR2140-1.1

orities revealed significant disagreements. These disagreements could stem from three sources: (1) differences in how people define the scope of the threats and hazards, (2) misconceptions about or incomplete awareness of the impacts of threats or hazards, and (3) genuine disagreement about the seriousness of the impacts of the threats and hazards.

Normatively, the first two of these sources of disagreement are not desirable. They are artifacts of judgments made when people have different definitions of the threats and hazards being assessed or facts about them. However, the third source of disagreement, differences in values among people and groups, is important to include in risk management deliberations.

The first several steps of the Deliberative Method for Ranking Risks were designed based on two principles. First, judgments about comparable risk should be informed by a common and consistent description of the impacts of threats and hazards that is informed by the best available information. Second, the descriptions must address all aspects of the threats and hazards that influence judgments of the risk associated with their impacts. If followed, these principles are intended to ensure that risk management deliberations are based on a common, valid understanding of the risks being managed. Evaluations of the Deliberative Method for Ranking Risks demonstrated that using these approaches to define and describe threats and hazards can reduce undesired disagreement, capture true disagreements based on differences in value judgments, and produce results that are considered valid and that provide reliable input to a risk management policy deliberation (Florig et al., 2001; Morgan et al., 2001; Willis et al., 2004; Willis et al., 2010; Lundberg and Willis, 2015; Lundberg and Willis, 2016). The process used for the HSNRC leveraged the aspects of the Deliberative Method for Ranking Risks related to defining and describing threats and hazards.

Each step in the risk assessment process is summarized in the remainder of this section and described in further detail in the subsequent chapters. The four steps of this process are supported by stakeholder engagement, which we describe first.

Key Supporting Activity: Engage Stakeholders

A key activity running through the entirety of the risk assessment methodology is stakeholder engagement. Continuous stakeholder engagement is intended to ensure that the scope of the HSNRC reflects the priorities of DHS offices and components, and to provide opportunity for review and commentary on the development of the methodology and the use of data to inform the analysis.

The Risk ESC and the TWG were both established to support the current risk assessment process. Early in the project, the RAND team conducted interviews with members of the TWG to understand perspectives on the HSNRC across DHS, including the perceived importance of recommendations made in prior reviews of HSNRC and QHSR, as well as to elicit additional concerns and recommendations for HSNRC.

During these interviews, TWG members confirmed that uncertainty remains within DHS about the purpose and scope of the HSNRC. They also suggested that the dissemination of methods and results from the HSNRC could be improved. Most had only seen a slide presentation concerning the first HSNRC, did not read the final product, and were unsure of where to find it. Some noted that having fewer people see the final document can result in a lower-quality product and reduce the impact of the results. It was also felt that limiting the use of For Official Use Only or classified analysis could increase distribution.

TWG members also suggested that the next HSNRC will need to harmonize risk approaches across DHS offices and components. Many were unaware of what data feed into the HSNRC risk analysis and whether their work would be consistent with the HSNRC purpose. Further, TWG members noted that DHS components view risk in different ways, which can result in different methodologies for risk analysis and diverse points of emphasis or focus. TWG members confirmed that a common strategy for comparing risk of different types was lacking.

The TWG and Risk ESC held meetings approximately monthly from April 2016 through March 2017 throughout the development of the risk assessment methodology.

Step 1. Select Threats and Hazards

This step has three parts: generating a list of threats and hazards to be considered, selecting screening criteria, and using the criteria to select a prioritized set of hazards.

Part 1: Generate a list of threats and hazards. The first part is to generate an initial list of hazards for consideration. The development of this list should be guided by DHS's strategic perspective, informed by prior risk analyses, and selected through deliberation among DHS components and offices.

Part 2: Select screening criteria. The second part is to screen hazards based on an agreed-upon set of criteria. The criteria should reflect the intended purpose of the risk assessment for the organization conducting it. The HSNRC used the following screening criteria, guided by the purpose of the strategic analysis and input from the Risk ESC:

- Is the threat or hazard exogenous to the homeland security enterprise?[2]
- Is the threat or hazard the result of either discrete events or persistent phenomena, not events that affect threats and hazards (e.g., climate change, which could change exposures to flooding and hurricanes) or are the effects of hazard (e.g., loss of a fishery)?
- Is the threat or hazard related to DHS strategic priorities as identified in department-level strategy and planning documents, particularly the prior QHSR?

---

2   The HSNRC did not include threats or hazards that are a result of the enterprise's structure, budgets, and oversight, each of which would be relevant to an enterprise risk assessment.

- Is DHS charged with mitigating the risks from the threat or hazard, in either a lead or major supporting role?
- Does the threat or hazard have the potential for significant impact on at least one of the following: (1) health, safety, and security; (2) the economy; (3) the natural environment; and (4) governance?

Part 3: Select a set of threats and hazards. The third part of the threat and hazard identification step is to use the screening criteria to select a set of hazards and threats for consideration.

Step 2. Select Risk Attributes

The attributes used to describe threats and hazard shape the characterization of how threats or hazards affect the nation. This step involves two parts. The first is determining a set of broad criteria for risk attributes, and the second is applying the criteria in selecting the attributes.

Part 1: Select criteria for risk attributes. Risk attributes should be selected using the following screening approach. This approach was designed to reflect the range of potential effects by focusing on four types of operationally relevant impacts: (1) health, safety, and security; (2) economic; (3) environmental; and (4) governance. To ensure attributes' usefulness within the HSNRC, each attribute should also be

- *measurable*, meaning that attributes are conceptually clear enough so that measures can be defined to describe the nature and extent of impacts
- *operationally relevant*, meaning that information to describe threats and hazards is available within the time and resource constraints of the HSNRC.

Furthermore, attributes should describe the uncertainty about threats and hazards.

The set of attributes as a whole should also balance three criteria: completeness, uniqueness, and conciseness. *Completeness* is needed to ensure that the full range of attributes is considered in setting priorities for risk management. *Uniqueness* is important to ensure that each attribute reflects a distinctive dimension of risk, that is, to avoid "double counting" of risk impacts. *Conciseness* helps facilitate analysis, thus ensuring that the information in the risk assessments can be used to support decisionmaking. The number of attributes should be as few as possible, since it is often easier to make comparisons or decisions when fewer dimensions are analyzed.

Part 2: Select attributes. The criteria from Part 1 are used to select risk attributes. In the current iteration, we first used completed comparative risk assessments to identify possible attributes that might be used to describe threats and hazards in the HSNRC. Then, starting from the list of possible attributes, we identified a set of the smallest number of attributes that would also meet the criteria of completeness, uniqueness, and conciseness while representing the dimensions addressed in prior risk assessments.

Step 3. Collect Data on Threats and Hazards

The next step in the methodology is to collect data on the selected threats and hazards. To describe threats and hazards using the attributes identified in Step 2, we requested data from the relevant DHS components during August 2016. Upon receiving data in response to the initial data call, we reviewed the completeness of the data and identified data gaps with the Risk ESC. In some cases, we were able to obtain additional data to address gaps using sources referenced in government-provided data, other government-published reports, or other published data identified through an online search of literature published in peer-reviewed journals, news media, and industry reports.

It should be noted that we had access to source material that documented analysis of components of the previous HSNRC, but we did not have a consolidated document describing the prior HSNRC methodology in its entirety. The current HSNRC drew on the 2011 Strategic National Risk Assessment (SNRA) documentation files held by DHS Policy (DHS, Office of Policy, no date), an overview briefing of the 2012 HSNRC (DHS, 2014a), the 2015 SNRA results that built on the prior analyses (DHS, 2014b), and the 2014 Flows study conducted in support of the 2014 QHSR (DHS, no date). Because of the absence of a published documentation of the HSNRC methodology, it was not possible to recreate the analysis conducted for the prior HSNRC in its entirety.

Step 4. Characterize Threats and Hazards

The inputs from the first three steps are used to characterize the threats and hazards and produce vetted risk summary sheets to inform discussion of risk management priorities. The risk summary sheets should be written in a consistent manner to describe

- the scope of the threat or hazard
- the mechanisms though which the threat or hazard affects the nation
- the impacts from the threat and hazard to the nation
- the uncertainty surrounding the likelihood and impacts associated with the threat or hazard.

The goal of the risk summary sheets is to provide, in a consistent manner, DHS and its partners across the homeland security enterprise with an overview of how each threat and hazard affects the nation. This overview can serve as a common foundation for analysis of homeland security risks to the nation and identification of priorities for managing them.

However, we note that developing the risk summary sheets involves considerable subjective input. An important part of developing the risk summary sheets, and therefore also of the HSNRC methodology, involves deciding *how* to describe the impacts of threats and hazards. Each risk summary sheet must consider how prior assessments were interpreted when making assessments for each attribute and provide citations for the assessments used. To make assessments for quantitative attributes, summary sheet authors must translate reviewed literature into order-of-magnitude assessments. To make assessments for qualitative attributes, authors should use reviewed literature to make an assessment of each threat and hazard, place it within a defined category of impact, and translate these defined categories into units of low, medium, or high. Chapter Three describes the approach used to make these judgments for the HSNRC in each impact category, and the reasoning behind the judgments made is documented in the risk summary sheets.

A risk summary sheet should be developed for each of the threats and hazards selected in Step 1. Risk summary sheets are organized by impact category.

Summary Risk Format. Each risk summary sheet begins with an overview that defines the particular threat or hazard being assessed. It is followed by an overview table, which contains estimates of the impacts of the threat or hazard in terms of all the attributes selected in Step 2 of the process. Table 1.1 shows a sample of the overview table. Following the overview table, each risk summary sheet is organized into several sections that provide an overview of the nature of the threat and hazard, the assessment of its impacts, and the rationale for these assessments. These sections are as follows:

- **Exposure and Effects.** This section provides an extended introduction that describes unique aspects of the nature of the exposure to the hazard in the United States, the manner in which consequences are manifest, and (as appropriate) factors that influence assessment of the impacts from the threat or hazard across impact attributes.
- **Health, Safety, and Security Impact.** The next section of the risk summary sheet addresses the health, safety, and security impact category and presents data on *Deaths, Injuries and Illnesses, and National Well-Being*, as described in Chapter Three in the section titled "Definitions and Measurement Approaches for Health, Safety, and Security Attributes." An example of coding the applicability of factors affecting well-being is shown in Table 3.3. The categorical scales for assessing national well-being/loss of confidence in societal and personal health, safety, and/ or security are found in Table 3.4.
- **Economic Impact.** Economic impact is divided into the attributes of *Economic Damages* (average annual and greatest impact in single episode) and *Greatest Critical or Lifeline Infrastructure Effects from a Single Episode*. The first attribute, as described in Chapter Three, is assessed using data from the literature. Table 3.5 provides the categorical scales for assessing disruption of critical or lifeline infrastructure effects.
- **Environmental Impact.** The attribute *Greatest Environmental Damage in a Single Episode* is used to assess environmental impact. This is estimated using a constructed, qualitative scale that accounts for the geographic extent of damage and time required to remediate the effects and reflects the greater of the impacts to species and ecosystem services (Table 3.6).

Table 1.1
Sample Overview Table: Summary Risk Characteristics

Characteristic	Estimates of Impact		
Health, Safety, and Security Impact			
Deaths	Low	Best	High
Average annual			
Greatest number in single episode			
Injuries and illnesses	Low	Best	High
Average annual			
Greatest number in single episode			
National well-being: loss of confidence in societal and personal health, safety, or security	(See Tables 3.3 and 3.4)		
Economic Impact			
Economic damages ($)	Low	Best	High
Average annual impact			
Greatest impact in a single episode			
Greatest critical or lifeline infrastructure effects from a single episode	(See Table 3.5)		
Environmental Impact			
Greatest environmental damage in a single episode	(See Table 3.6)		
Governance Impact			
Greatest disruption of National Essential Functions in a single episode	(See Table 3.7)		
Frequency, Predictability, and Precision of Estimates			
Frequency of occurrence			
Predictability of event	(See Table 3.8)		
Precision of estimate	(See Table 3.9)		

- **Governance Impact.** *Greatest Disruption of National Essential Functions in a Single Episode* is the attribute used to assess governance impact. The assessment considers the eight National Essential Functions (Federal Emergency Management Agency [FEMA], 2017) across two dimensions: population affected and duration. The Categorical Scales for Assessing Disruption of National Essential Functions are found in Table 3.7.
- **Frequency, Predictability, and Precision of Estimates.** These attributes are assessed as follows:

- *Frequency* describes how regularly the threat of hazard typically occurs somewhere in the United States and is described categorically, with estimates ranging from as frequent as *daily* to as infrequent as *once a millennium.*
- *Predictability* is measured by the extent to which the expected impact of a threat or hazard can be forecasted. It is assessed using two unrelated factors that each influence the ability to forecast a threat. The first is the extent to which warning can be provided for any single episode. The second is the quality of (or level of confidence) in sources from which an annual impact can be estimated. The categorical scales for assessing predictability are shown in Table 3.8.
- *Precision* is assessed categorically with values of low, medium, and high based on the ranges of estimates for average annual fatalities, injuries, and economic damage. For each of these categories, the number of orders of magnitude spanning the low, best, and high estimates is summed and scored, as shown in Table 3.9.

To ensure the consistency and quality of the summary sheets, they were subjected to DHS and independent expert reviews that considered three factors:

- First, was the risk assessment approach applied consistently across threats and hazards?
- Second, were the data sources appropriate, given available information about the threats and hazards?
- Finally, were the assessments in the risk summary sheets consistent with supporting information?

Limitations

Implementation of the risk assessment methodology was constrained by several factors. It is important to consider the implications of these factors when using the resulting risk summary sheets for strategic planning purposes.

First, our data collection for this effort was deliberately prescribed. All data were either provided by DHS components or found through literature searches by the RAND team. We did not extend the data call to other government agencies with equities in risk management for the selected threats and hazards. For example, we did not reach out to the Federal Bureau of Investigation for information related to terrorism, and we similarly did not reach out to the Drug Enforcement Administration or the Office of National Drug Control Policy on transnational drug trafficking information. In cases like these, we relied only on reports we found online from these organizations, as well as other relevant studies found through literature searches.

In cases where TWG or Risk ESC members did not reference prior studies, we attempted to find data sources on our own. The sources identified were subsequently reviewed by members of the TWG and Risk ESC for completeness and quality. Recommendations from these reviews identified additional data sources. However, our data sources were not reviewed by other U.S. government departments or external technical experts in the fields related to the threats and hazards.

The identified sources did not fill all data gaps. Many of the data used are historical. Data gaps remained, especially for threats and hazards that have not been observed. For example, some terrorism scenarios have not occurred and thus are not reflected in historical records. Additional gaps remained for threats that are difficult to measure, such as human trafficking or other illegal activities. In these cases, there were either very few sources or no sources upon which to make assessments of the impact of threats and hazards on the nation. As a result, uncertainty about some threats and hazards remains great. The basis of assessments and resulting uncertainty is documented in the risk summary sheets.

Second, the majority of TWG members did not participate in the process leading up to the 2014 QHSR, and few were aware of the GAO or after-action review findings on the QHSR. Thus, while the TWG's participation was helpful, members were not able to provide insights into the previous process used or to make specific assessments of how well the new process addresses issues identified regarding prior processes.

Third, expert judgment is inherently subjective. Even with a repeatable, transparent process, one cannot ensure that a different group of stakeholders using the same process at a different time would arrive at the same decisions this group of stakeholders did (e.g., about which threats and hazards to include). For the HSNRC, we implemented two measures to facilitate the repeatability of results, given current policy priorities, organizational structure, and legal authorities at DHS:

- Engagement with the DHS Risk ESC: We implemented this process with consistent engagement with the DHS Risk ESC. This committee comprised representatives from each of the department's operational components and major headquarters offices. The committee was organized by DHS Policy, and its members were selected by the participating organizations. Engagement of this group is intended to ensure that the HSNRC results reflected perspectives of professionals from across DHS.
- Iterative review of results: At each step of the process described in this chapter, results were reviewed iteratively with members of the Risk ESC or designees on the TWG of this committee. Iterative review provides opportunity for DHS components and offices to point out where the risk assessment does not reflect the scope of DHS strategies and missions or is not consistent with available information.

Together, these two measures were intended to help ensure that perspectives from all organizations across DHS were considered and that variations in judgments due to selection of specific individuals could be balanced by review and discussion of the group.

If a future assessment sought to evaluate the repeatability of the results, several other approaches might be used to provide expert judgment. For example, the process could be implemented using multiple review committees from across DHS and comparing results across these groups. Alternatively, collection of feedback on interim reviews could incorporate more elaborate and structured elicitation approaches, such as a formal Delphi process (Brown, 1968). However, each of these approaches would require additional efforts from across the department.

Finally, the collaborative process added another layer of complexity. Incorporating feedback and stakeholder perspectives, including those of RAND team members, and input from DHS, frequently required multiple iterations and attempts to synthesize multiple viewpoints. We made recommendations about how particular decisions should be resolved, but final decisionmaking rested with government stakeholders.

Organization of This Report

The remainder of this report describes the implementation of this process for the HSNRC and is organized in five chapters and four appendixes:[3]

- Chapter Two describes selection of threats and hazards to be included in the HSNRC.
- Chapter Three describes selection of risk attributes.
- Chapter Four describes the process of writing risk summary sheets describing the threats and hazards.
- Chapter Five presents our conclusions and discusses the ways in which risk assessment information informs risk management and decisionmaking.
- The appendixes present our draft lists of threats and hazards, definitions of the final set of threats and hazards, the literature reviewed, and the attributes identified during the literature review.

---

[3]   The full set of risk summary sheets is presented in a separate volume that is not available to the public.

CHAPTER TWO

Selecting Threats and Hazards

The first step in developing the risk assessment methodology is to document how threats and hazards are to be selected for inclusion. Selecting hazards to be included is inherently a subjective decision. Therefore, it is important to design a process that is transparent and repeatable. The decision is made within the context of current priorities and competing objectives. Consequently, the threats and hazards that are considered most important today may differ from those that are considered most important in the future because of changes in priorities and objectives.

This chapter describes selection of threats and hazards to include in the 2017 HSNRC. It then presents a list of current threats and hazards that resulted from using this process. As described in Chapter One, the goal of the HSNRC is to describe a set of strategically relevant threats and hazards posing significant risk to the nation that DHS must manage. Selecting threats and hazards for the HSNRC can help DHS understand which threats and hazards pose the greatest risk and can assist DHS in identifying the greatest opportunities for further reducing risk.

The threats and hazards covered in the HSNRC are not intended to provide a comprehensive list of issues affecting the nation but must meet specific screening criteria relevant to the requirements for the HSNRC, as discussed later in the chapter. DHS is required by authority and statute to address many threats and hazards that were not included in the HSNRC, such as interdiction of illegal fishing or support or assistance to communities following wildfires. Exclusion of such threats and hazards from the HSNRC does not indicate priorities for budgeting and resourcing. It simply indicates that the threat or hazard was judged to not meet the criteria for inclusion in the HSNRC.

We followed the three-part process described in Chapter One:

- Part 1: Generate a list of threats and hazards
- Part 2: Select screening criteria
- Part 3: Select a set of threats and hazards.

The process also includes extensive stakeholder review and feedback on each of these steps. This process resulted in selection of the 28 threats and hazards listed in Table 2.1 (shown at the end of the chapter) for inclusion in the HSNRC.

Part 1: Generation of a List of Threats and Hazards for the HSNRC

The process of identifying threats and hazards for the HSNRC was guided by strategic perspective and informed by prior analyses. To generate the list of threats and hazards, we first reviewed the 2014 QHSR to identify DHS's stated strategic priorities. For 2014, these priorities were

- securing against the evolving terrorism threat
- safeguarding and securing cyberspace
- countering biological threats and hazards
- securing and managing flows of people and goods
- strengthening the execution of DHS missions through public-private partnerships.

Ideally, the process of identifying threats and hazards would include engagement with leadership across DHS to identify additional strategic priorities. In lieu of this engagement strategy, we amended the set of threats and hazards identified by our review of the QHSR with the sets of threats and hazards captured in three other sources:

- overviews of the 2014 HSNRC
- the 2015 *Strategic National Risk Assessment*
- a review by DHS Policy of threats and hazards that were not considered in the 2014 HSNRC but could be included in the 2017 HSNRC.

These documents contained an overlapping set of 85 threats and hazards for consideration (see Tables A.1 and A.2, respectively).

We viewed the 2014 QHSR and other assessments as collectively reflecting threats and hazards previously identified as being salient to leadership across DHS. However, we did not include all the threats and hazards from these sources individually, but, in some cases, combined related threats and hazards into an aggregated category. For example, while prior analyses included several scenarios related to biological terrorism, in the current set we included all these scenarios as a single category of threat. We combined threats and hazards when possible to develop a list that was comprehensive but that avoided overlap across threats and hazards to the extent possible. The final list was intended to be a minimum comprehensive list that included 15 threats and 19 hazards (see Tables A.3 and A.4, respectively). It was presented for review to DHS Policy, the

TWG, and the Risk ESC during June 2016, along with the process for screening hazards presented later in this chapter,

Part 2: Selection of Screening Criteria for the HSNRC

To match the intended goal of focusing the HSNRC on strategically significant risks to the United States, we established criteria for determining which threats and hazards have significant enough consequences to merit inclusion in the HSNRC. In developing these criteria, we considered critiques of the 2014 HSNRC and incorporated feedback from the TWG and Risk ESC.

The resulting decision proposed to and approved by the Risk ESC and TWG was that the 2017 HSNRC would include only threats and hazards that are exogenous to the homeland security enterprise and that represent discrete events or persistent phenomena. That is, we would not include threats or hazards that are a result of the enterprise structure, budgets, and oversight (i.e., factors that are relevant to an enterprise risk assessment), nor would we include the effects of a threat or hazard as an item to be assessed (e.g., loss of a fishery as opposed to illegal fishing) or factors that modify hazards over time (e.g., climate change, which could change exposures to flooding and hurricanes).

We also applied three additional screening criteria for determining threats and hazards, shown in Figure 2.1.

Guided by the authorizing legislation for the QHSR, we defined these screening criteria as follows:

- *Related to DHS strategic priorities* refers to being identified in department-level strategy and planning documents, particularly the prior QHSR. Inclusion in a component-level strategy and planning document does not necessarily require inclusion

Figure 2.1
Screening Criteria for Selecting Threats and Hazards

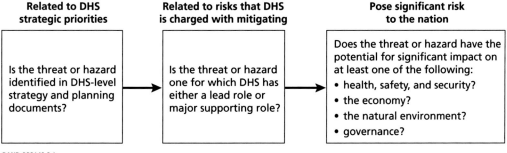

- *Related to risks that DHS is charged with mitigating* refers to threats or hazards for which DHS has either a lead role or major supporting role
- *Pose significant risk to the nation* means that the set of threats and hazards includes reasonable scenarios that would have an impact on one or more of the following (FEMA, 2017):
  - health, safety, and security: leads to deaths, injuries, suffering, or a breakdown in public safety requiring a response beyond that provided by local authorities
  - economic activity: leads to property damage and economic disruption that spans geographic regions and/or economic sectors
  - environment: leads to damage to the ecosystem and its flora, fauna, and functions that will affect a region for a time frame longer than a few months
  - governance: leads to disruptions of any of the eight National Essential Functions.

These criteria were proposed by RAND and accepted by the TWG and ESC. We screened potential threats and hazards for inclusion in the HSNRC based on whether or not the criteria applied.

Part 3: Selection of a Set of Threats and Hazards for Inclusion in the HSNRC

The process of selecting a set of threats and hazards for assessment involved ongoing stakeholder engagement with the TWG and the Risk ESC. We solicited written comments from DHS Policy and the TWG on both the broader set of threats and hazards proposed for consideration and the application of the screening criteria and selection of hazards for the HSNRC. Based on this input, we revised the proposed threat and hazard set and presented the results to the Risk ESC. In cases where consensus was lacking on whether to include or exclude a particular threat or hazard, DHS Policy made the final decision.

Selection of the final set of threats and hazards began with the refined set of threats and hazards contained in Tables A.3 and A.4. By assessing each threat and hazard using the screening criteria described in the last section, we concluded that eight threats and 15 hazards met all the screening criteria (see Table A.5). The complete assessments upon which these judgments are based are available for review as well.

We presented the initial list of threats and hazards to the TWG, who discussed the list and provided follow-up comments. Four components provided comments— the DHS Office of Operations Coordination, the Domestic Nuclear Detection Office, the National Protection and Programs Directorate, and the U.S. Coast Guard. We revised the list to reflect discussion and recommendations. Key revisions included the following:

- Consideration of six additional threats and hazards
  - Two were assessed to meet the screening criteria: radiological attack and mass migration.
  - Four were assessed to not meet the screening criteria: human trafficking, international money laundering, heat waves, and urban conflagration.
- Revision of assessments for some screening factors based on component inputs, including considering psychological impact as part of the health, safety, and security impact screening factor, which led to the inclusion of terrorist large-scale small arms/explosives attacks.
- Modification of the names of several threats and hazards to clarify the scope of what was included.

The revised draft list of threats and hazards (shown in Appendix Table A.4) was presented to the Risk ESC. The Risk ESC discussion was inconclusive, and the list was remanded to the TWG for further discussion.

Based on TWG discussion and component input, we made further revisions to the list at the direction of DHS Policy, significantly:

- inclusion of human trafficking, reflecting a recommendation by the U.S. Citizenship and Immigration Service and DHS Policy that it should be considered to have the potential for significant impact on health, safety, and security
- inclusion of drought, based on FEMA recommendation that DHS be recognized as having a significant role in mitigating the associated risk
- inclusion of wildfire, based on FEMA recommendation that DHS be recognized as having a significant role in mitigating the associated risk
- modification of the scope of drug trafficking to be transnational drug trafficking to emphasize the significant DHS interdiction role in addressing countering illegal drugs
- aggregation of all infrastructure failure/accident hazards into a single hazard, based on National Protection and Programs Directorate recommendation, called technical failure or industrial accident.

Discussions with the TWG and Risk ESC revealed general consensus on most items on the list, with several issues outstanding. As a result, DHS Policy decided to include counterfeit goods in response to U.S. Customs and Border Protection's recommendation that DHS be recognized as having a significant role in mitigating the associated risk. DHS Policy also decided not to include cyber attacks that steal private-sector data (because of lack of clarity on the resulting impacts and on the DHS role) and immigration benefit fraud and abuse (because of lack of clarity on the distinction in impacts from those of terrorism and illegal migration).

The final list of threats and hazards approved for inclusion in the HSNRC is shown in Table 2.1. Appendix B provides definitions for each of the approved threats and hazards.

Table 2.1
Final List of Threats and Hazards Approved for Inclusion in the Homeland Security National Risk Characterization

Terrorist Threats

- Attack on leadership
- Attacks targeting critical infrastructure
- Biological weapon attack
- Chemical weapon attack
- Nuclear attack
- Radiological attack
- Small arms/explosive attack on populations

Cyber Threats

- Cyber attack on critical infrastructure networks
- Cyber attack that steals sensitive government data
- Cyber attack on government networks

Illegal Activities

- Counterfeit goods
- Human trafficking
- Illegal migration
- Mass migration
- Transnational drug trafficking

Natural Hazards

- Drought
- Earthquake
- Flooding
- Hurricane
- Space weather
- Tsunami
- Volcano
- Wildfire

Health Hazards

- Agricultural plant disease outbreak
- Foreign animal disease outbreak
- Transnational communicable disease

Infrastructure Hazards

- Technical failure or industrial accident of critical infrastructure caused by human error or age

Other

- Electromagnetic pulse

CHAPTER THREE

Selecting Risk Attributes

The next step in the risk assessment methodology is to select the risk attributes, that is, the criteria to be used in characterizing the potential impact of the chosen threats and hazards. As noted previously, the HSNRC should describe threats and hazards in a consistent way. The selection of attributes provides a transparent means of categorizing the types of risks posed by specific threats and hazards, as well as the nature and extent of uncertainty about the threats and hazards.

This chapter begins by describing a set of criteria, proposed by RAND and accepted by the TWG, that define in broad terms the characteristics of a good set of risk attributes; these criteria apply to all the attributes. Next, we describe the process of selecting the specific set of attributes identified for the HSNRC. The selected attributes were used to describe the impacts of the selected threats and hazards, as well as the level of uncertainty surrounding those estimates.

Part 1: Selection of Criteria for Risk Attributes

The threats and hazards in the homeland security domain listed in Table 2.1 can affect the nation in many ways. The screening approach used to select threats and hazards for the HSNRC (see Chapter Two) reflected the range of potential effects through its focus on four types of impacts from these threats and hazards:

- health, safety, and security
- economic
- environmental
- governance

As a set, attributes used to describe threats and hazards should cover all of these four impact categories.

However, there are also many potential ways to measure and describe the impacts of threats and hazards for each of these four broad categories. Health impacts can be measured using many dimensions of morbidity and mortality. Economic impact can be measured in terms of property damage and disrupted economic activity, including both direct and indirect effects. Environmental impacts can include effects on animals, plants, ecosystem services, and aesthetics. Governance impacts can be described across a similarly broad set of outcomes, ranging from loss of confidence in government and related services to severe societal disruption. Each of these dimensions can be represented using a unique attribute.

However, this could potentially result in a list of attributes too large to be useful. Therefore, we used the criteria described in Chapter One to select attributes that are each *measurable* and *operationally relevant* while as a set being *complete, unique,* and *concise.*

Part 2: Selection of Risk Attributes

The approach used to select risk attributes included two steps.

First, we identified possible attributes that might be used to describe threats and hazards in the HSNRC. We did this by first reviewing completed comparative risk assessments with similar scope or purpose to the HSNRC (listed in Appendix C) and compiling a list of all the attributes used. These studies included almost 100 different attributes that had been used for assessing risk. The full list of attributes we extracted from this literature is provided in Appendix D.

A one-for-one relationship does not always exist between an attribute and its associated impact category. For example, damage to ecology was identified as having an environmental impact. However, it most likely also has an economic impact. In this case, since the primary impact was assessed to be environmental, it was identified in this category rather than as an economic impact.

Second, starting from the list of all possible attributes, we identified a subset of attributes while balancing the criteria of completeness, uniqueness, and conciseness and also representing the dimensions addressed in prior risk assessments. Selecting the subset of attributes involved discussions with the TWG and Risk ESC about possible sets of attributes. The discussions also covered the proposed approach for evaluating the impacts of threats and hazards using the proposed attributes. Selection of attributes was also informed by our initial attempts to use the attributes to evaluate the impacts of the selected threats and hazards.

The iterative discussions about selecting a subset of attributes highlighted several issues that were ultimately incorporated into the selected attributes, including the need to

- address effects on perceptions of well-being that may motivate attention by government independent of the magnitude of other types of impacts
- account for the effects of infrastructure disruptions that may not be well captured in analyses of economic impacts

- ensure that the value-of-life is not double-counted by inclusion in both health impacts and economic impacts[1]
- define governance impacts as disruptions of National Essential Functions (at the recommendation of DHS Policy and FEMA)
- describe the frequency of occurrence of the threats and hazards
- address select aspects of uncertainty surrounding the impacts described with selected attributes
- reflect both the cumulative annual impact of occurrence of threats and hazards, as well as the potential for high impacts from specific scenarios.

The description of attributes in the next section explains how each of these issues was ultimately resolved. The Risk ESC approved the final set of attributes.

Selected Set of Attributes for Describing Consequences and Uncertainty

We developed two sets of attributes for describing risk: one set to describe consequences of the threats and hazards, and another to describe uncertainty in the assessment of the threats and hazards.

Assessing Consequences

The attributes of consequences for describing risk from homeland security threats and hazards are listed in Table 3.1. Some of these attributes are easily amenable to quantitative measures (e.g., economic damage), and others require use of qualitative approaches (e.g., the selected attributes to describe effects on national well-being). Some attributes measure distinct concepts (e.g., fatalities), and others are constructed measures that aggregate several types of impact (e.g., environmental damage).

Addressing Uncertainty

Risk assessments using these attributes reflect uncertainty in two ways. First, for each of the attributes using a quantitative measure, descriptions include low, best, and high estimates for that attribute. Second, the three attributes in Table 3.2—frequency, predictability, and precision—can be used to describe other dimensions of the uncertainty surrounding threats and hazards, since these characteristics also influence risk perceptions and decisions about risk management. The approach used to measure each proposed attribute is described in the next section.

---

[1]   We excluded the value-of-life from economic impacts since we included deaths and injuries as health and safety attributes.

Table 3.1
Final Set of Attributes of Consequences for Describing Risk in the Homeland Security National Risk Characterization

Impact Category	Attribute	Units
Health, Safety, and Security	Deaths	Number of deaths, described as average per year and greatest number in a single episode
	Injuries and illnesses	Number of injuries and illnesses, described as average per year and greatest number in a single episode
	National well-being Loss of confidence in societal and personal health, safety, and/or security	Qualitative assessment of the expected impact on perceptions that government can provide desired security, described as average annual impact and greatest impact in a single episode (low, medium, high)
Economic	Economic damages	Dollars, described as average annual impact and greatest impact in a single episode
	Greatest critical or lifeline infrastructure effects from a single episode	Qualitative constructed scale reflecting duration and number of affected customers (low, medium, high)
Environmental	Greatest environmental damage in a single episode	Qualitative constructed scale accounting for effects on species, ecosystems, and viewscapes that reflects time required for remediation and geographic extent of damage (low, medium, high)
Governance	Greatest disruption of National Essential Functions in a single episode	Qualitative constructed scale accounting for the population affected and duration of disruptions (low, medium, high)

Table 3.2
Final Set of Attributes of Uncertainty for Describing Risk in the Homeland Security National Risk Characterization

Attribute	Units
Frequency of occurrence	Description of frequency ranging from daily to millennially
Predictability	Constructed, qualitative scale reflecting the amount of warning for a single episode and the ability to estimate annual impacts (low, medium, high)
Precision	Qualitative aggregated assessment of precision in estimates across all attributes

Definitions and Measurement Approaches for Health, Safety, and Security Attributes

In this section, we briefly define the attributes shown in Tables 3.1 and 3.2.

Deaths Per Year

The *average number of deaths per year* is the expected number of deaths per year among residents in the United States (excluding U.S. territories) from current levels of exposure to the hazard (i.e., the residual risk). For events that typically occur less frequently than annually, this value represents the expected value of an event occurring in any year. For this attribute, the best estimate reflects the expected annual losses from the threat or hazard and the low and high estimates reflect uncertainty surrounding the average annual losses.

The *greatest number of deaths in a single episode* is the greatest number of people who might be killed in a single event involving a given hazard. For this attribute, and others that consider the greatest impact from a single episode, impact is estimated as being an extreme event that could be used for the basis of contingency planning, that is, a reasonable worst case but not the absolute worst case possible. Assessment of this "worst-case" impact does not consider a single scenario. Rather, the assessment considers the range of events that could occur in the range of worst-case estimates. Thus, for some threats and hazards, a range of worst-case impacts are considered. Estimates of deaths could be based either on historical data, modeling, intelligence estimates, or other documented expert judgment.

Injury and Illness

Injuries and illnesses reflects nonfatal health consequences from the threat or hazard. Injuries vary in both duration and severity. This includes more-severe injuries or illnesses and less-severe injuries or illnesses. More-severe physical injuries or illnesses are typically defined as ones requiring hospitalization, while less-severe injuries or illnesses may be treated at a hospital but not admitted. Both more-severe and less-severe injuries include both short-term and long-term consequences. Similar to fatalities, this attribute is estimated for both the *average annual impacts* and the *greatest number expected for a single episode* using a variety of types of data.

National Well-Being

Impacts on national well-being measures the widespread perceptions among the public that the government is unable to provide for safety or security by preventing events from happening following the occurrence of a threat or hazard. There are no existing approaches to measure, directly and quantitatively, the expected impacts of threats or hazards on national well-being. As a result, the approach used to assess loss of well-being captures only some aspects of well-being and is inherently subjective. It is intended, however, to differentiate threats and hazards based on one aspect of well-being: *loss of confidence in societal and personal health, safety, and/or security.*

The public can lose confidence for many reasons. The public could fear that future events cannot be prevented, that they cannot be protected from them, or that the government will not respond effectively should an event occur. Fear is not the only emotion that could lead to loss of confidence. Anger, frustration, or impatience could also lead to a loss of confidence.

Studies of risk perceptions suggest that several factors influence these perceptions. Some of those factors involve characteristics of people exposed. For example, studies of reactions to terrorism have shown that risk perceptions varied based on how connected individuals are to an attack based on personal exposure, social connectedness to those affected, and geographic proximity. Furthermore, these perceptions change as time passes following an event (Fischhoff et al., 2003; Burns, Peters, and Slovic, 2012).

Other factors that affect perceptions involve characteristics of the threats or hazards (Slovic, Fischhoff, and Lichtenstein, 1985). For example, fear tends to be greater when (1) the event in question is not common and well understood, (2) the event is perceived to be indiscriminate in who it affects and requires taking extreme measures (such as moving or severely curtailing common daily activities) to avoid being affected, (3) the event is associated with lack of information about events that limit one's ability to avoid being affected as events are occurring, and (4) people hold a belief that the government is not able to respond as it should to the event. These factors are coded as "yes," "no," or "in some cases," and summarized in Table 3.3

Increased fear can contribute to loss of confidence at the individual level. However, when perceptions are widespread, they can lead to effects at the societal level. The attribute for well-being tiers threats or hazards based on how many of these four factors were judged to apply to a threat or hazard.

This attribute could in theory be estimated for both the *average annual impact* and the *greatest impact from a single episode.* The greatest impact from a single episode is evaluated using a qualitative scale that reflects assessments of this attribute in risk summary sheets. Each threat or hazard is assessed on whether each factor affecting

Table 3.3
Applicability of Factors Affecting Well-Being

Factor	Possible Codes
Event uncommon and not well understood creating fear of unknown	Yes/No/In some cases
Event is perceived to be indiscriminate in who it affects and requires taking extreme measures to avoid exposure	Yes/No/In some cases
Event is associated with lack of information about events or how to avoid being affected as events are occurring	Yes/No/In some cases
Event could create a belief that the government is not able to respond effectively	Yes/No/In some cases

well-being is applicable to the threat or hazard based on a review of collected risk assessments and scenario assessments. These assessments are documented in the risk summary sheets. Then, threats and hazards are binned into low, medium, and high categories based on the number of factors judged to apply to the threat or hazard using the following rating scheme (Table 3.4).

When considering the average annual impact, assessments of the threats and hazards resulted in no threats and hazards being assessed to meet the characteristics that promote fear on a regular basis. Rather, they were judged to do so only when the events happen in a large episode. This resulted in all ratings being low and no variation across threats and hazards. For this reason, the risk summary sheets do not describe the average annual impacts on well-being.

Definitions and Measurement Approaches for Economic Attributes

Economic Damage

Economic damage is measured by the expected economic consequences that result from destruction of property, business disruption, and indirect impacts that result from changes in consumption patterns among residents and firms, as well as steps both take in efforts to be resilient in the wake of events. For events that typically occur less

Table 3.4
Categorical Scales for Assessing National Well-Being/Loss of Confidence in Societal and Personal Health, Safety, and/or Security

Number of Factors	Rating
0	None
0–1	None to Low
1	Low
1–2	Low to Medium
2	Medium
2–3	Medium to High
3	Medium to High
3–4	High
4	High

NOTE: When a factor is rated as uncertain depending on circumstances of the range of reasonable worst-case scenarios, this uncertainty is reflected with ratings of 0–1, 1–2, 2–3, or 3–4 accordingly.

than once a year, this value represents the expected value of an event occurring in any year. The economic value of life is not included, as morbidity and mortality impacts are recorded using separate attributes under the category of health, safety, and security impacts. Economic damages are described in terms of both the *average damages per year* and the *greatest economic damage in a single episode.*

Greatest Critical or Lifeline Infrastructure Effects from a Single Episode

This attribute describes the potential for disruption of critical infrastructure services (e.g., electricity or commercial aviation) estimated qualitatively with three levels of low, moderate, and high disruption. These categories are presented using constructed scales across two dimensions: *number of effected customers* and *duration. Number of affected customers* indicates how many people are affected by the disruption. In urban areas, the number of affected customers would reside in a smaller geographic area than in rural areas. *Duration* reflects expected length of the disruption. Both numbers affected and duration have categories of low, moderate, and high according to the criteria in Table 3.5 and assessments made based on interpretation of available literature about the threats and hazards.

Definitions and Measurement Approaches for Environment and Governance Attributes

Greatest Environmental Damage in a Single Episode

This is defined in terms of impacts on species and ecosystem services. This is estimated using a constructed, qualitative scale that accounts for the geographic extent of damage and time required to remediate the effects and reflects the greater of the impacts to species and ecosystem services (see Table 3.6). *Geographic extent* distinguishes those events that affect smaller areas (city- or county-level), areas similar to small to large states, or

Table 3.5
Categorical Scales for Assessing Disruption of Critical or Lifeline Infrastructure Effects

Duration	Customers Affected		
	Low (<100,000)	Moderate (100,000–1 million)	High (>1 million)
High (>1 month)	Medium	High	High
Moderate (1 week–1 month)	Low	Medium	High
Low (<1 week)	Low	Low	Medium

NOTE: Assessments for impacts on infrastructure are made by assessing the impacts on two factors, customers affected and duration, as indicated in this table and assigning the associated impact level of low (green), medium (yellow), or high (red).

Table 3.6
Categorical Scales for Assessing Environmental Damage

Remediation Period	Geographic Extent		
	Low (city or county)	Moderate (state)	High (region or nation)
High (>1 decade)	Medium	High	High
Moderate (1 year–1 decade)	Low	Medium	High
Low (<1 year)	Low	Low	Medium

NOTE: Assessments for environmental impacts are made by assessing the impacts on two factors, geographic extent and duration, as indicated in this table and assigning the associated impact level of low (green), medium (yellow), or high (red).

areas spanning several large states to the nation as a whole. *Remediation period* reflects the duration expected for the effects to be viewed as addressed. As with the greatest number of deaths, this is estimated as being an extreme event. As with other estimates of the greatest impact, these impact estimates could be based either on historical data, modeling, or intelligence estimates. Environmental damage is considered categorically, with low, medium, and high damage according to the criteria in Table 3.6 and assessments made based on interpretation of available literature about the threats and hazards.

Greatest Disruption of National Essential Functions in a Single Episode

This describes the extent to which the eight critical governmental services, as defined by Presidential Policy Directive 40 and FEMA's Continuity Guide (October 2013), are disrupted. The eight National Essential Functions (FEMA, 2017) are as follows:

1. Ensure the continued functioning of our form of government under the Constitution, including the functioning of the three separate branches of government.
2. Provide leadership visible to the nation and world.
3. Defend the Constitution against all enemies and preventing or interdicting attacks against the United States, its people, property, or interests.
4. Maintain and fostering relationships with foreign nation.
5. Protect against threats to the homeland and bringing to justice perpetrators of crimes.
6. Provide rapid and effective response to and recovery from incidents.
7. Protect and stabilizing the nation's economy.
8. Provide for critical federal government services that address the national health, safety, and welfare of the United States.

This attribute is assessed into categories of low, medium, and high using constructed scales to assess the worst overall impact across these eight services considering two dimensions in Table 3.7: *population affected* and *duration*. Both population and duration have categories of low, moderate, and high, and assessments for each dimension were made based on interpretation of available literature about the threats and hazards. *Population affected* indicates how many people are affected by the disruption. In urban areas, this number would reflect a smaller geographic extent than in rural areas. *Duration* reflects expected length of the disruption. As with estimates of the greatest impact for fatalities, injuries, and economic damages, this represents the impacts from an extreme event that is a reasonable worst case, but not the absolute worst case possible. These impact estimates could be based either on historical data, modeling, or intelligence estimates.

Definitions and Measurement Approaches for Attributes of Frequency, Predictability, and Precision

Frequency of Occurrence

This attribute describes how regularly the threat of hazard typically occurs somewhere in the United States. Regularly occurring hazards occur in episodes that can be observed every day. For events that occur regularly, frequency can be informed by historical data. For those that are rare, or perhaps have never happened, frequency can be described using modeling or expert judgment. Literature cited in the HSNRC uses all of these approaches, depending on the threat or hazard. Frequency is described categorically, ranging from estimates of daily to as infrequent as once a millennium. Where uncertainty exists, ranges are used.

Predictability

This attribute is measured by the extent to which the expected impact of a threat or hazard can be forecasted. This is assessed using a qualitative constructed scale that

Table 3.7
Categorical Scales for Assessing Disruption of National Essential Functions

Duration	Population Affected		
	Low (<100,000)	Moderate (100,000–1 million)	High (>1 million)
High (>1 month)	Medium	High	High
Moderate (1 week–1 month)	Low	Medium	High
Low (<1 week)	Low	Low	Medium

NOTE: Assessments for disruption of National Essential Functions are made by assessing the impacts on two factors, population affected and duration, as indicated in this table and assigning the associated impact level of low (green), medium (yellow), or high (red).

reflects two unrelated factors that each influence the ability to forecast a threat. The first is the extent to which warning can be provided for any probable worst-case episode. The second is the quality of (or level of confidence) in sources from which an annual impact can be estimated considering all of the types of impacts. Threats and hazards are assessed on each of these dimensions and binned into categories of low, medium, and high using the matrix in Table 3.8.

Precision

The measure for this attribute is designed to reflect the overall uncertainty across estimates of all impacts related to health, safety, and security and economic damage. It is assessed categorically with values of low, medium, and high. Assessments are based on the ranges of estimates for average annual fatalities, injuries, and economic damage. For each of these categories, the number of orders of magnitude spanning the low, best, and high estimates is calculated. For example, if the low and high estimates are both ten, the range is zero orders of magnitude. However, if the low is tens and the high is thousands, the range is two orders of magnitude. These ranges are then added together to give a combined uncertainty number. If a ratio cannot be calculated because estimates are unknown, then the precision is estimated to be low. The thresholds for low, moderate, and high are derived from the data so that the hazards are distributed based on observed thresholds across the hazard set according to values provided in Table 3.9. Precision in the estimates is distinct from accuracy and also should not be mistaken with levels of confidence in judgments.

Table 3.8
Categorical Scales for Assessing Predictability

	Warning		
Quality of Source	**Low (no warning)**	**Moderate (hours of warning)**	**High (days or more of warning)**
High (government, academic, or other known and reliable source)	Medium	High	High
Moderate (source of unknown or questionable reliability)	Low	Medium	High
Low (source of known low reliability, or no external source)	Low	Low	Medium

NOTE: Assessments for predictability are made by assessing the impacts on two factors, quality of source and warning, as indicated in this table and assigning the associated impact level of low (red), medium (yellow), or high (high).

Table 3.9
Scoring Rules for Assessing Precision of Estimates

Total Orders of Magnitude Across Impact Categories	Precision Rating
0–2	High
3–4	Medium
5–6	Low
Unknown	Low

CHAPTER FOUR

Data Collection and Characterization of Threats and Hazards

This chapter focuses on the final two steps in the risk assessment methodology: collection of data on threats and hazards, and the characterization of threats and hazards in the risk summary sheets.

Although the process used to characterize risks and hazards builds on the foundation described in this report so far, its implementation was complex, requiring ongoing collaboration and multiple iterations involving members of the RAND team, frequently in consultation with the TWG and the Risk ESC. Application of the risk assessment methodology to specific threats and hazards in the risk summary sheets typically required several judgments to be made, given that there were many issues left open to interpretation and, in many cases, a lack of data that could be used to fully address those issues.

The data collection and risk characterization process followed a common approach for each threat/hazard. This approach (explained further below) included an initial data search conducted by the team, a data call to DHS, supplementary efforts to address data gaps, and development of the risk summary sheet template to use in writing the risk characterization for each threat/hazard.

Overview of Approach Used for Data Collection and Characterization of Threats and Hazards

Assessments of threats and hazards were made based on review of literature that described the types of scenarios associated with each threat and hazard, the impacts and likelihood of the scenarios, and (if available) national risk assessments of the threat or hazard. This literature was identified by DHS through interactions with the Risk ESC and members of the TWG committees. The body of assessments identified through this consultation was augmented through literature reviews conducted by members of the RAND study team.

In developing the risk summary sheets, we began by reviewing the 2014 QHSR and other existing data for each of the selected threats and hazards. Our goal was to synthesize existing assessments rather than to conduct new primary research and analysis.

We developed a data collection plan for each threat and hazard and conducted an initial data search based on that plan. We then requested data from relevant DHS components. We reviewed the completeness of the data received and identified any data gaps, which we reviewed with the TWG and the DHS Risk ESC. DHS Policy assisted in addressing data gaps, where possible. RAND team members sought out additional open-source government data to attempt to fill gaps.

We used the selected attributes described in Chapter Three to develop a template for the risk summary sheets to ensure that the risk characterizations used a consistent approach. The assessment addressed both the likelihood and consequences of risks. The completed summary sheets are provided in a separate volume.

While these steps provide a consistent framework that was used in the risk characterization, the dynamics of the process played out in sometimes complex ways, as described further below.

Data Collection

RAND developed a data collection plan that was designed to incorporate completed risk assessments that address the likelihood, vulnerability, and consequences associated with selected threats and hazards. In the plan, we defined a completed analysis as one that

- provides integrated analysis, not simply raw data, which addresses likelihood, vulnerability, and consequences, or as many of these three components as possible in a single document
- focuses on risk within the next five years
- is national- or sector-level analysis, rather than scenario-specific analysis
- was produced by a U.S. government agency or other generally recognized source, such as an academic institution.

This definition provided a basic means of assessing the data sources received to determine their adequacy for contributing to the risk characterization.

We began data collection by conducting our own search for relevant open-source assessments. The 2015 SNRA was the starting point for data collection, although it did not address all threats and hazards included in the HSNRC. The documents found during these initial searches provided a useful, if incomplete, set of data on which to develop the risk summary sheets. In some cases, such as the assessment of natural disaster hazards, the data collected from these initial searches ultimately provided as many as half the citations used in the final risk characterization.

Following our initial data collection activities, we requested data from relevant DHS components. We reached out to members of the TWG for assistance in identifying and obtaining completed risk analyses to supplement the initial data we identified. We asked our DHS Policy contact to request data from DHS components, as appropriate. As described previously, this data call focused only on DHS, because there was not an established interagency mechanism to coordinate the data request. For this reason, the process relied on DHS offices to be aware of and recommend analyses that existed in other parts of the government.

For the data call, we identified DHS offices or components that were expected to have the most access to and awareness of relevant risk analyses. Through the TWG, we asked components to review this information and provide feedback regarding additional DHS components that might have relevant analyses, suggest other relevant materials that they could not provide directly but for which they could identify a specific source, and provide any documents, information, or sources believed to be relevant.

This process identified a number of open-source documents related to the threats and hazards. The data cited in assessing each threat or hazard are listed for each risk summary sheet.

Review and Analysis of Data Collected

We encountered several challenges with the data provided. We found that these materials did not cover all of or map exactly to the selected threats and hazards. We also found that the amount and quality of data varied across threats and hazards. Few of the assessments were supported by models of broad sets of scenarios, and few assessments incorporated national-level broad scenario analysis based on historical analysis. Further, the data did not fully address all the selected attributes. Notable gaps include impacts on well-being and governance.

We reported on the data gaps to the TWG and ESC and asked for additional help in addressing the gaps, which DHS Policy facilitated. While this process was able to address some gaps, in many cases there were gaps that could not be entirely addressed.

Characterization of Threats and Hazards in the Risk Summary Sheets

Applying the risk assessment methodology consistently across a diverse set of threats and hazards was challenging. To maintain consistency, the full range of attributes across all the threats and hazards on all risk summary sheets were applied. In some cases, however, this meant that it was necessary to describe impacts that were not associated with the particular threat or hazard or that were judged to be very low. For example, deaths are not typically associated with agricultural plant disease outbreaks, and environmental impacts are not associated with transnational communicable disease outbreaks. Including all attributes in each assessment, despite the apparent limited relevance in some cases, allows for subsequent comparisons of threats and hazards to each other.

In other cases, application of attributes consistently across threats and hazard required describing attributes relevant to episodic threats to be judged as low for threats for which the cumulative impact is most relevant. For example, crimes such as human trafficking and transnational drug trafficking are generally thought to affect a few people at a time, but over the course of a year can result in large cumulative impacts.

In many cases, assessing impacts of specific attributes for a threat or hazard was challenging because of the data gaps described previously. In these cases, judgment was required on how best to interpret the limited data that were available. In some cases (e.g., many of the cyber-related threats), data were so limited that impacts were listed as unknown. In other cases (e.g., crimes such as the health impacts of counterfeit goods), judgments were made based on a limited number of sources that document impacts. In still other cases (e.g., environmental impacts from attacks on critical infrastructure), literature provided only a description of the phenomenon through which impacts could result and this information was used as the basis of judgments.

Finally, several of the attributes relied on qualitative, subjective assessments to categorize impacts as low, medium, or high. This approach was used when assessing impacts on well-being, infrastructure disruption, the environment, and governance. A similar approach was also used to assess the predictability of threats and hazards. To increase the reliability of the assessments, we established the structured approaches for assessing impacts of these attributes that are described in Chapter Three. Still, application of this approach required judgment and introduced subjectivity.

The approaches used to address each of these issues required judgments. To maintain transparency in the HSNRC, where such judgments were made, the risk summary sheets document the approach taken, rationale for the approach, and literature cited. As described in Chapter One, the risk assessment process involved subjecting the draft risk summary sheets to review by experts at DHS identified by the Risk ESC as well as experts at RAND independent of the study team that implemented the HSNRC. The RAND reviewers are listed in the acknowledgments section.

CHAPTER FIVE

Conclusion: How Risk Assessment Informs Risk Management

The results of the HSNRC presented in this report were motivated by three goals. First, DHS required a transparent and repeatable process for assessing and comparing strategically significant threats and hazards from which DHS is responsible for protecting the nation. Once developed and demonstrated, this process could serve as a part of the foundation for DHS strategic planning. The documentation contained in this report can assist DHS in repeating and advancing this approach with future strategic planning efforts.

Second, risk assessments produced using the HSNRC process can serve as a common reference point for discussions about how these threats and hazards affect the nation. Together, the risk summary sheets contained in an accompanying volume to this report describe the landscape of threats and hazards that DHS is responsible for managing.[1] Because the threats and hazards are described in a consistent manner, they can be used to answer several questions for DHS leadership about the nature of homeland security risks to the nation:

- What threats pose the greatest risks, by type of impact? For example, which threats have the greatest potential for economic disruption, kill the most people each year, and are judged to have the greatest impact on well-being?
- What patterns exist across categories of impact? For example, which threats or hazards could have large, infrequent episodic impacts but are poorly understood; and which have well-defined, large cumulative impacts on a regular basis?
- What threats or hazards need to be better understood before we can decide how to act? For example, which have the widest variance in expected impact or are the least predictable?

Third, a common understanding of the impacts of threats and hazards on the nation would assist DHS leadership in developing and implementing strategic plans that direct the department's resources to achieve the desired approach to protecting the

---

[1] A forthcoming report reviews the assessments documented in the risk summary sheets and identifies insights on the homeland security risk landscape that the leadership of DHS should be aware of.

nation from threats, responding to disasters, and promoting economic resilience. This strategy could identify

- opportunities to mitigate risk further: ways in which additional resources would fill a recognized gap in homeland security capabilities
- problems for which new approaches are needed to mitigate risk: innovative solutions in areas where existing approaches are deemed ineffective or inefficient
- issues for which more information is needed to guide strategy: topics that require further analysis before decisions can be made about how to respond to the problem or whether a response is needed at all.

The HSNRC does not provide all information required to complete this strategic planning effort. Steps required to provide additional perspectives that would be required to build from risk assessment to risk management include the following:

- *Understand which threats and hazards pose the greatest risk to the nation.* Prioritizing risks requires judgments about the relative importance of different categories of impact. If such a prioritization is desired, risks could be prioritized using a deliberative process that captures judgments of DHS leadership informed by the shared perspective on threats and hazard contained in the risk summary sheets. The HSNRC provides the factual information with which to have these discussions.
- *Identify threats and hazards for which current efforts are disproportionate to risk.* Assessing the appropriateness of current resource decisions requires prioritization of risks. However, it also requires information about how DHS employs its resources. Details of DHS programming and budgeting, with respect to the HSNRC threats and hazards, could identify areas where the level of effort for risk management seems too high or too low, given the level of risk posed to the nation.
- *Provide recommendations on how to further reduce risk.* Risk management priorities depend on more than how big risks are and how much effort is being directed toward them. Decisions of how to further reduce risk require knowledge of what existing capabilities are, what perceived gaps exist, and the costs and effectiveness of potential solutions.
- *Place DHS's role and responsibilities within the larger context of whole-of-government responsibilities for managing the risks from the identified threats and hazards.*

Other supporting DHS strategic analyses provide this information. By combining the results of the HSNRC with the complementary analyses of DHS authorities, programming, capabilities, and gaps, DHS will be able, if desired, to sort the homeland security risk landscape into problems that are understood well enough and problems that need to be better understood. Similarly, it would be possible to sort the risk landscape into problems for which more can be done and those for which enough is already being done. With insights like these, the department could form the foundation for DHS strategic planning and resource guidance.

Draft Lists of Recommendations for Threats and Hazards to Be Included

This appendix provides draft lists of recommendations for threats and hazards to be included in the 2017 HSNRC. Table A.1 includes threats and hazards included in the 2013 HSNRC. Table A.2 includes additional threats and hazards proposed in the DHS after-action review of the 2013 HSNRC. Table A.3 provides RAND's initial draft recommendations for threats, while Table A.4 provides RAND's initial draft recommendations for hazards. Table A.5 provides a revised list of recommendations for both threats and hazards. The final approved list of threats and hazards is shown in Table 2.1.

Table A.1
Threats and Hazards Included in the 2013 Homeland Security National Risk Characterization

Quantitative Plots of Frequencies and Consequences	Qualitative Narrative
<ul><li>Accidental biological food contamination</li><li>Accidental chemical substance spill or release</li><li>Accidental radiological substance release</li><li>Aircraft as a weapon</li><li>Animal disease outbreak</li><li>Armed assault</li><li>Biological terrorism attack, nonfood</li><li>Chemical terrorism attack, nonfood</li><li>Chemical/biological food contamination terrorism attack</li><li>Cyber events that impede system operations</li><li>Cyber events that extract or alter information without system impacts</li><li>Dam failure</li><li>Disruptive strike/industrial action</li><li>Drought</li><li>Earthquake</li><li>Explosives terrorism attack</li><li>Extreme cold/snowstorm</li><li>Flood</li><li>Heat/heat wave</li><li>Human pandemic outbreak</li><li>Hurricane</li><li>Illegal immigration</li><li>Illicit drugs</li><li>Industrial accidents, explosions</li><li>Mass migration</li><li>Large oil spills</li><li>Nuclear terrorism attack</li><li>Pipeline failure</li><li>Power grid failure</li><li>Radiological terrorism attack</li><li>Small oil spills</li><li>Transportation system failure</li><li>Tornado</li><li>Urban conflagration</li><li>Wildfire</li></ul>	<ul><li>Cyber events that extract or alter information without system impacts</li><li>Cyber: crippling cascading attack on critical infrastructure</li><li>Cyber: data destruction results in degraded commercial viability or government service</li><li>Cyber: distributed denial of service (DDOS) attack causes erosion of consumer confidence and economic loss</li><li>Space weather</li><li>Tsunami</li><li>Volcano eruption</li></ul>

Table A.2
Future Threats and Hazards from the After Action Review of the 2013 Homeland Security National Risk Characterization

- Biological/bacterial drug resistance
- Child exploitation
- Civil disorder: mass riot/protest/occupy demonstration
- Civil liberty risks (e.g., false negative or false positive identification)
- Climate change
- Climate change, progressive
- Commercial fraud
- Counterfeit goods (including pharmaceuticals)
- Counterterrorism/joint terrorism task force (JTTF)
- Detention facility overcrowding/overcapacity
- Dignitary threats
- Drug shortage
- Drug smuggling
- Electromagnetic pulse
- Emerging Infections human diseases
- Encroachment on trade zones
- Enterprise risk resulting from fiscal problems
- Events requiring search and rescue
- Financial crimes (including counterfeiting)
- Global or domestic market/economy fluctuation
- Fisheries depletion
- Fossil fuel dependence/shortage
- Gang activity from illegal immigrant communities
- Domestic gang activity
- General smuggling
- Harm to species
- Human smuggling
- Human trafficking
- Identity and immigration benefit fraud
- Illegal exports of controlled materials
- Illegal plant/food stuff
- Illegal workers (worksite enforcement)
- Infrastructure aging/degradation
- Intellectual property theft
- Interoperable communications failure
- Maritime accidents
- Plant disease outbreak
- Strategic/counterproliferation
- Summaries of individual regional Threat and Hazard Identification and Risk Assessments (THIRAs) and state/urban area/tribal assessments
- Theft of government material
- Transportation system failure
- Use of fraudulent documents and admissions
- Water security/resources

Table A.3
RAND Initial Draft Recommendations for Threats to Be Included in the 2017 Homeland Security National Risk Characterization

Type of Threat	Recommended for Inclusion	Not Recommended for Inclusion
Terrorist threats	• Nuclear attack • Biological weapon attack • Chemical weapon attack • Leadership attack • Infrastructure attack (e.g., railways, airplane/airport, bridges, dams, refineries)	• Electromagnetic pulse • Coordinated, large-scale small arms/explosive attack
Cyber threats	• Critical infrastructure attack damaging or disrupting large portion of infrastructure sector • Destruction/degradation of critical U.S. government systems or data	• Massive disruption of financial sector/markets
Transnational criminal threats	• Illegal migration	• Drug trafficking • Counterfeit goods • Currency counterfeiting • Illegal fishing

Table A.4
RAND Draft Initial Recommendations for Hazards to Be Included in the 2017 Homeland Security National Risk Characterization

Type of Threat/Hazard	Recommended for Inclusion	Not Recommended for Inclusion
Natural hazards	• Earthquake • Tsunami • Hurricane • Volcano • Space weather • Flooding	• Drought • Winter storm • Windstorm • Wildfire
Health hazards	• Transnational communicable disease • Food animal disease outbreak • Agricultural plant disease outbreak	
Infrastructure hazards	• Power grid failure • Maritime oil spill • Nuclear plant failure • Chemical facility accident • Dam failure • Pipeline failure	

Table A.5
Revised Draft Recommendations for Threats and Hazards to Be Included in the 2017 HSNRC Presented to the Risk ESC

Type of Threat/Hazard	Recommended for Inclusion	Not Recommended for Inclusion
Terrorist threats	• Nuclear attack • Radiological attack • Biological weapon attack • Chemical weapon attack • Leadership attack • Large-scale small arms/explosive attack • Infrastructure attack (e.g., railways, airplane/airport, bridges, dams, refineries)	• Electromagnetic pulse
Cyber threats	• Critical infrastructure attack affecting large portion of infrastructure sector • Destruction/degradation of critical U.S. government systems or data	• Massive disruption of financial sector/markets
Transnational criminal threats	• Illegal migration (via human smuggling)	• Drug trafficking • Human trafficking • International money laundering
Other illegal activities	• Mass migration	• Counterfeit goods • Domestic currency counterfeiting • Illegal foreign fishing
Natural hazards	• Earthquake • Tsunami • Hurricane • Volcano • Space weather • Flooding	• Drought • Winter storm • Windstorm • Wildfire • Heat wave • Urban conflagration
Health hazards	• Transnational communicable disease • Food animal disease outbreak • Agricultural plant disease outbreak	
Infrastructure hazards	• Power grid failure • Maritime oil spill • Nuclear plant failure • Chemical facility accident • Dam failure • Pipeline failure	

Definitions of Threats and Hazards

This appendix provides definitions of the final set of threats and hazards.

Table B.1
Definitions of Threats and Hazards

Threat/Hazard	Definition
Terrorist Threats	
Attack on critical infrastructure[1]	A terrorist attack in the United States involving the use of physical infrastructure as a weapon or as a target to attack civilians or noncombatants in manner to increase the deaths, injuries, economic damage, or fear that results from the event. Examples include attacks involving any of the 16 critical infrastructure sectors identified in Presidential Policy Directive 21.
Attack on leadership	A terrorist attack in the United States targeting a government official, such as the President, Vice President, members of Congress, Supreme Court judges, federal Cabinet-level appointments, and foreign heads of state visiting the United States.
Small arms or explosives attack	A terrorist attack in the United States involving use of firearms or explosives that targets civilians or noncombatants. Types of events include those perpetrated by lone actors, small groups, or large coordinated groups.
Biological weapon attack	A terrorist attack in the United States involving use of biological material on civilian targets.
Chemical weapon attack	A terrorist attack in the United States involving use of chemical material on civilian targets.
Nuclear attack	A terrorist attack in the United States involving use of nuclear device on civilian targets.
Radiological attack	A terrorist attack in the United States involving use of radiological material on civilian targets.
Cyber Attacks	
Cyber attack on critical infrastructure networks[1]	An attack by a criminal, hacktivist, terrorist group, or nation-state on information technology networks that destroys, denies, degrades, or disrupts; manipulates users of; or damages infrastructure in either a designated lifeline sector (energy, transportation, communications, and water and wastewater) or the financial services sector.
Cyber attack on government networks	An attack by a criminal, hacktivist, terrorist group, or nation-state on or using information technology networks that destroys; denies, degrades, or disrupts; deceives users of; or damages a U.S. federal, state, or local civilian government network that supports government communication or delivery of government services.

Table B.1—continued

Threat/Hazard	Definition
Cyber attack that steals sensitive government data	An attack by a criminal, hacktivist, terrorist group, or nation-state on U.S. federal, state, or local government civilian computer networks that steals data that should be safeguarded for personal privacy, proprietary, or national security reasons. Thefts of sensitive government data from non-government (e.g., contractor) computer networks are also included.
Illegal Activities	
Counterfeit goods	The importation of goods that violate intellectual property rights as a result of the violation of patents, copyrights, and trademarks.
Human trafficking	The recruitment, transportation, transfer, harboring, or receipt of persons by means of the threat or use of force for the purpose of exploitation. Exploitation includes, at a minimum, prostitution of others or other forms of sexual exploitation, forced labor or services, slavery or practices similar to slavery, servitude, or the removal of organs.
Illegal migration	The entry into or unlawful presence of people in the United States in a manner that violates U.S. immigration laws. Illegal migration can result from entry without inspection between ports of entry, entry using fraudulent documents at a port of entry, or overstaying a legitimate entry visa.
Mass migration	The sudden movement of large groups of people into the United States from one geographic region. It generally results from people fleeing persecution or physical harm in such a magnitude and duration that it poses a threat to the national security of the United States as determined by the President. Mass migration is differentiated from illegal migration based on the volume, rate, and geographic nature of the migration.
Transnational drug trafficking	The movement of illicit drugs (including cocaine, heroin, marijuana, and methamphetamines) into the United States through ports of entry or between ports of entry for purposes of cultivation, manufacture, distribution, and sales. The impacts of drug trafficking do not include the effects of illicit drug use or of related criminal activities that transnational drug trafficking organizations may engage in.
Natural Hazards	
Drought	A "deficiency in precipitation over an extended period" relative to normal conditions for a given region. (National Oceanic and Atmospheric Administration [NOAA])
Earthquake	A violent shaking event that occurs without warning and can cause massive amounts of destruction over large geographic areas, including to structures above and below ground. (FEMA)
Flooding	"Any high flow, overflow, or inundation by water that causes or threatens damage." (National Weather Service)
Hurricane	An "intense tropical weather system[s] with a well defined circulation and maximum sustained winds of 74 mph (64 knots) or higher." (NOAA)
Space weather	"Variable conditions on the sun and in space that can influence the performance of technology" on earth. (FEMA)
Tsunami	A set of large ocean waves generated by underwater disturbances, including earthquakes, landslides, or volcanic eruptions. (NOAA)
Volcano	Cracks or vents in the earth's crust, often within a mountain, which can explode, releasing molten rock and poison gas, and producing flying rock and large volumes of ash. (FEMA)
Wildfire	An unwanted and unplanned nonstructure fire in an undeveloped area. (National Interagency Fire Center Communicator's Guide)

Table B.1—continued

Threat/Hazard	Definition
Health Hazards	
Agricultural plant disease outbreak	An outbreak of a plant pathogen or pest that has the potential to reduce or destroy plants so significantly that it results in a national-level event.
Foreign and emerging animal disease outbreaks	A terrestrial animal disease or pest, or an aquatic animal disease or pest, not known to exist in the United States or its territories, and thought to pose a significant threat. An *emerging animal disease* is any terrestrial animal, aquatic animal, or zoonotic disease not yet known or characterized, or any known or characterized terrestrial animal or aquatic animal disease in the United States or its territories that changes or mutates in pathogenicity, communicability, or zoonotic potential to become a threat to terrestrial animals, aquatic animals, or humans.
Transnational and multistate communicable disease	"The occurrence of cases of disease in excess of what would normally be expected in a defined community, geographical area or season. An outbreak may occur in a restricted geographical area, or may extend over several countries. It may last for a few days or weeks, or for several years." (World Health Organization)
Infrastructure Hazards	
Critical infrastructure failure caused by age or human error[a]	Critical infrastructure failure occurs when some element of a facility, physical asset, or engineered system is unable to perform as designed as a consequence of preventable causes, such as poor design, aging components, lack of adequate maintenance and repair, human error, or similar causes. For this assessment, the list of potential failure types consists of: • drinking water contamination • drinking water delivery failure • train crashes • airline crashes • bridge collapse • power outages • telephone service outages • 911 outages • Internet outages • chemical facility accidental release • hazmat releases from trains • pipeline rupture • maritime oil spill • dam/levee failure • nuclear plant failure.
Other	
Electromagnetic pulse	A short burst of electromagnetic energy, typically generated by a nuclear burst (which could occur, for example, as the result of a terrorist attack) that can damage electronic equipment.

[a] The infrastructure sectors covered in attacks on critical infrastructure varied across assessments of terrorist attacks on critical infrastructure, cyber attacks on critical infrastructure networks, and critical infrastructure failure. The sectors covered were chosen based on the nature of each threat or hazard and are described in the corresponding risk summary sheets.

Literature Consulted in the Identification of Potential Attributes to Describe Threats and Hazards

This appendix provides a list of works consulted in developing the approach for selecting attributes to describe threats and hazards, which is found in Chapter Three.

Abadie, A., and J. Gardeazabal, "The Economic Costs of Conflict: A Case Study of the Basque Country," *American Economic Review*, Vol. 93, No. 1, 2003, pp. 113–132.

Blomberg, S. B., and G. D. Hess, "Estimating the Macroeconomic Consequence of 9/11," *Peace Economics, Peace Science and Public Policy*, Vol. 15, No. 2, 2009, p. 7.

Blomberg, S. B., G. D. Hess, and A. Orphanides, "The Macroeconomic Consequences of Terrorism," *Journal of Monetary Economics*, Vol. 51, No. 5, 2004, pp. 1007–1032.

Chen, A. H., and T. F. Siems, "The Effects of Terrorism on Global Capital Markets," *European Journal of Political Economy*, Vol. 20, No. 2, 2004, pp. 349–366.

Collier, P., "On the Economic Consequences of Civil War," *Oxford Economic Papers*, Vol. 51, No. 1, 1999, p. 168.

Eckstein, Z., and D. Tsiddon, "Macroeconomic Consequences of Terror: Theory and the Case of Israel," *Journal of Monetary Economics*, Vol. 51, No. 5, 2004, pp. 971–1002.

Enders, W., G. F. Parise, and T. Sandler, "A Time-Series Analysis of Transnational Terrorism: Trends and Cycles," *Defence and Peace Economics*, Vol. 3, No. 4, 1992, pp. 305–320.

Federal Emergency Management Agency, *2011 Strategic National Risk Assessment*, Washington, D.C., 2011.

———, *2015 Strategic National Risk Assessment*, Washington, D.C., 2015.

Fielding, D., "Modelling Political Instability and Economic Performance: Israeli Investment During the Intifada," *Economica*, Vol. 70, No. 277, 2003, pp. 159–186.

Fleischer, A., and S. Buccola, "War, Terror, and the Tourism Market in Israel," in Yoel Mansfeld and Abraham Pizam, eds., *Tourism, Security and Safety: From Theory to Practice*, Oxford, UK: Elsevier/Butterworth-Heinemann, 2006.

Freudenburg, W. R., "Contamination, Corrosion and the Social Order: An Overview," *Current Sociology*, Vol. 45, No. 3, 1997, p. 19.

Frey, B. S., S. Luechinger, and A. Stutzer, "Calculating Tragedy: Assessing the Costs of Terrorism," *Journal of Economic Surveys*, Vol. 21, No. 1, 2007, p. 1.

Gordon, P., J. E. Moore, J. Y. Park, and H. W. Richardson, "The Economic Impacts of a Terrorist Attack on the US Commercial Aviation System," *Risk Analysis*, Vol. 27, No. 3, 2007, pp. 505–512.

Greenberg, M. R., M. Lahr, and N. Mantell, "Understanding the Economic Costs and Benefits of Catastrophes and Their Aftermath: A Review and Suggestions for the US Federal Government," *Risk Analysis*, Vol. 27, No. 1, 2007, p. 83.

Haimes, Y. Y., B. M. Horowitz, J. H. Lambert, J. Santos, K. Crowther, and C. Lian, "Inoperability Input-Output Model for Interdependent Infrastructure Sectors—II: Case Studies," *Journal of Infrastructure Systems*, Vol. 11, No. 2, 2005.

Homeland Security Council and U.S. Department of Homeland Security, *National Planning Scenarios*, Washington, D.C., 2005.

Homeland Security Presidential Directive 7, *Critical Infrastructure Identification, Prioritization, and Protection*, Washington, D.C.: The White House, 2003.

Ito, H., and D. Lee, "Assessing the Impact of the September 11 Terrorist Attacks on US Airline Demand," *Journal of Economics and Business*, Vol. 57, No. 1, 2005, pp. 75–95.

Keeney, R. L., and D. von Winterfeldt, "A Value Model for Evaluating Homeland Security Decisions," *Risk Analysis*, Vol. 31, No. 9, 2011, pp. 1470–1487.

Lindell, M. K., and C. S. Prater, "Assessing Community Impacts of Natural Disasters," *Natural Hazards Review*, Vol. 4, No. 4, 2003.

Lundberg, Russell, *Comparing Homeland Security Risks Using a Deliberative Risk Ranking Methodology*, Santa Monica, Calif.: RAND Corporation, PGSD-319, 2013. As of November 21, 2017:
https://www.rand.org/pubs/rgs_dissertations/RGSD319.html

Mileti, D. S., *Disasters by Design: A Reassessment of Natural Hazards in the United States*, Washington, D.C.: National Academies Press, 1999.

National Consortium for the Study of Terrorism and Responses to Terrorism, *Global Terrorism Database—Codebook: Inclusion Criteria and Variables*, College Park, Md.: University of Maryland, June 2017. As of November 21, 2017:
https://www.start.umd.edu/gtd/downloads/Codebook.pdf

National Research Council, Committee on Assessing the Costs of Natural Disasters, *The Impacts of Natural Disasters: A Framework for Loss Estimation*, Washington, D.C.: National Academies Press, 1999.

National Research Council, Committee on Assessing Vulnerabilities Related to the Nation's Chemical Infrastructure, *Terrorism and the Chemical Infrastructure: Protecting People and Reducing Vulnerabilities*, Washington, D.C.: National Academies Press, 2006.

National Research Council, Committee on Disaster Research in the Social Sciences: Future Challenges and Opportunities, *Facing Hazards and Disasters: Understanding Human Dimensions*, Washington, D.C.: National Academies Press, 2006.

National Research Council, Committee on Risk Characterization, *Understanding Risk: Informing Decisions in a Democratic Society*, Washington, D.C.: National Academies Press, 1996.

National Research Council, Committee to Review the Department of Homeland Security's Approach to Risk Analysis, *Review of the Department of Homeland Security's Approach to Risk Analysis*, Washington, D.C.: National Academies Press, 2010.

Norwood, A. E., R. J. Ursano, and C. S. Fullerton, "Disaster Psychiatry: Principles and Practice," *Psychiatric Quarterly*, Vol. 71. No. 3, 2000, pp. 207–226.

Nitsch, V., and D. Schumacher, "Terrorism and International Trade: An Empirical Investigation," *European Journal of Political Economy*, Vol. 20, No, 2, 2004, pp. 423–433.

Picou, J. S., B. K. Marshall, and D. A. Gill, "Disaster, Litigation, and the Corrosive Community," *Social Forces*, Vol. 82, No. 4, June 2004.

Rose, A., J. Benavides, S. E. Chang, P. Szczesniak, and D. Lim, "The Regional Economic Impact of an Earthquake: Direct and Indirect Effects of Electricity Lifeline Disruptions," *Journal of Regional Science*, Vol. 37, No. 3, 1997, pp. 437–458.

Rose, A., K. Porter, N. Dash, J. Bouabid, C. Huyck, J. Whitehead, D. Shaw, R. Eguchi, C. Taylor, and T. McLane, "Benefit-Cost Analysis of FEMA Hazard Mitigation Grants," *Natural Hazards Review*, Vol. 8, No. 4, 2007.

Rose, A., and S. Y. Liao, "Modeling Regional Economic Resilience to Disasters: A Computable General Equilibrium Analysis of Water Service Disruptions," *Journal of Regional Science*, Vol. 45, No. 1, 2005, pp. 75–112.

Rose, A. Z., "A Framework for Analyzing the Total Economic Impacts of Terrorist Attacks and Natural Disasters," *Journal of Homeland Security and Emergency Management*, Vol. 6, No. 1, 2009.

Rose, A., and D. Lim, "Business Interruption Losses from Natural Hazards: Conceptual and Methodological Issues in the Case of the Northridge Earthquake," *Global Environmental Change B: Environmental Hazards*, Vol. 4, No. 1, 2002, pp. 1–14.

Tierney, K., "Impacts of Recent Disasters on Businesses: The 1991 Midwest Floods and the 1994 Northridge Earthquake," in Barclay G. Jones, ed., *Economic Consequences of Earthquakes: Preparing for the Unexpected*, Buffalo, N.Y.: MCEER Publications, 1997.

Travalio, G. M., "Terrorism, International Law, and the Use of Military Force," *Wisconsin International Law Journal*, Vol. 18, No. 1, 2000, pp. 145–192.

Treverton, G. F., J. L. Adams, J. Dertouzos, A. Dutta, S. S. Everingham, and E. V. Larson, "The Costs of Responding to the Terrorist Threats: The US Case," in Philip Keefer and Norman Loayza, eds., *Terrorism, Economic Development, and Political Openness*, Cambridge, UK: Cambridge University Press, 2008, pp. 48–80.

U.S. Department of Homeland Security, " The 2014 Quadrennial Homeland Security Review," no date. As of November 21, 2017:
https://www.dhs.gov/sites/default/files/publications/qhsr/the-2014-quadrennial-homeland-security-review-overview.pdf

———, *National Infrastructure Protection Plan*, Washington, D.C., 2009.

———, *Homeland Security National Risk Characterization*, Washington, D.C., 2014.

U.S. Department of Homeland Security, Risk Steering Committee, *DHS Risk Lexicon*, Washington, D.C., 2008.

Willis, H. H., M. L. DeKay, M. G. Morgan, H. K. Florig, and P. S. Fischbeck, "Ecological Risk Ranking: Development and Evaluation of a Method for Improving Public Participation in Environmental Decision Making," *Risk Analysis*, Vol. 24, No. 2, 2004, pp. 363–378.

Willis, H. H., J. MacDonald Gibson, R. A. Shih, S. Geschwind, S. Olmstead, J. Hu, A. E. Curtright, G. Cecchine, and M. Moore, "Prioritizing Environmental Health Risks in the UAE," *Risk Analysis*, Vol. 30, No. 12, 2010, pp. 1842–1856.

Attributes Identified Through Literature Review

Appendix Table D.1 shows the full list of attributes identified in the literature for each of the four impact categories.

Table D.1
Attributes Identified in Literature, Organized by Impact Category

Impact Category	Attributes Identified in Literature
Health, Safety, and Security	Mortality-related • Average number deaths per year • Greatest number deaths in single episode • Average number of deaths in single episode • Total deaths Morbidity-related • Injuries per event or annually • Combined injuries/illnesses per event (range) • More serious injuries or illnesses per year (average) • Less serious injuries or illnesses per year (average) • Illnesses per event or annually • Disabilities • Quality-adjusted life year • Disability-adjusted life year • Severity of injury • Length of injury • Total injuries/illness Fear- and insecurity-related • Psychological impact • Psychological harms per year on average • Psychological health • Psychological—general • Distress • Fear • Depression • Other stress related psychological harms • Loss of societal cohesion • Loss of confidence in government Societal harms • Average individuals displaced per year • Average displaced households per year • Historical maximum displacement per event • Historical average displacement per event • Historical lowest displacement per event • Homelessness • Demographic changes • Crime • Drug addiction • Disruption of society • Degradation of social fabric • Degradation of lifestyle • Degradation of families • Community cohesion • For all Americans: search, privacy, movement • For subsets of Americans: unequal treatment, stereotyping • Restrictions on freedoms/rights • Loss of public morale/confidence

Table D.1—continued

Impact Category	Attributes Identified in Literature
Economic	Average economic damages per year
	Greatest economic damages in single episode
	Property damage
	Duration of economic damages
	Direct economic consequences
	Size of area affected by economic damages
	Businesses affected
	Houses destroyed
	Families/individuals loss of income
	Business disruption
	Damage to critical infrastructures
	Indirect economic damage
	Regional economic impact
	Sector economic impact (e.g., airlines, tourism)
	National economic impact
	Stock/capital market effects
	Savings switching to consumption
	Non-market damage (e.g., historic sites)
	Encroachment on U.S. territory/Exclusive Economic Zone
	Increased government expenditures
	Jobs lost
	Unemployment
Environmental	Damage to ecology
	Human impacts—including agriculture
	Aesthetic impacts
	Flora affected
	Fauna affected
	Water/land/air impacts
	Average environmental damage per year
	Environmental
Governance	Disruption of government events
	Provision of essential government services
	Mission disruption
	Loss of public order
	Government continuity
	Reduced emergency response
	Status of alliances
	Global leadership
	International relations
Other	Ability of an individual to control his or her exposure
	Time between exposure and health effect
	Quality of scientific understanding
	Natural/human-induced
	Combined uncertainty
	Frequency
	Likelihood

References

Brown, Bernice B., *Delphi Process: A Methodology Used for the Elicitation of Opinions of Experts*, Santa Monica, Calif.: RAND Corporation, P-3925, 1968. As of November 21, 2017: https://www.rand.org/pubs/papers/P3925.html

Burns W. J., E. Peters, and P. Slovic, "Risk Perception and the Economic Crisis: A Longitudinal Study of the Trajectory of Perceived Risk," *Risk Analy*sis, Vol. 32, No. 4, 2012, pp. 659–677.

DHS—*See* U.S. Department of Homeland Security.

Federal Emergency Management Agency, *Continuity Guidance Circular 2 (CGC 2): Continuity Guidance for Non-Federal Governments: Mission Essential Functions Identification Process (States, Territories, Tribes, and Local Government Jurisdictions)*, Washington, D.C., FEMA P-789, October 2013. As of December 5, 2017: https://www.fema.gov/media-library-data/1384435934615-7eeac7d0b4f189839f396a3c64eeac7a/ Continuity_Guidance_Circular_2.pdf

———, "List of National Essential Functions," 2017. As of November 21, 2017: https://emilms.fema.gov/IS547A/COOP0102080text1.htm

FEMA—*See* Federal Emergency Management Agency.

Fischhoff, B., R. M. Gonzalez, D. A. Small, and J. S. Lerner, "Judged Terror Risk and Proximity to the World Trade Center," *Journal of Risk and Uncertainty*, Vol. 26, Nos. 2–3, 2003, pp. 137–151.

Florig, H. K., M. G. Morgan, K. M. Morgan, K. E. Jenni, B. Fischhoff, P. S. Fischbeck, and M. L. DeKay, "A Deliberative Method for Ranking Risks (I): Overview and Test Bed Development," *Risk Analysis*, Vol. 21, No. 5, 2001, pp. 913–921.

GAO—*See* U.S. Government Accountability Office.

Lundberg, R., and H. H. Willis, "Assessing Homeland Security Risks: A Comparative Assessment of Ten Hazards," *Homeland Security Affairs*, Vol. 11, Article 10, December 2015.

———, "Deliberative Risk Ranking to Inform Homeland Security Strategic Planning," *Journal of Homeland Security and Emergency Management*, Vol. 13, No. 1, 2016, pp. 3–33.

Morgan K. M., M. L. DeKay, P. S. Fischbeck, M. G. Morgan, B. Fischhoff, and H. K. Florig, "A Deliberative Method for Ranking Risks (II): Evaluation of Validity and Agreement Among Risk Managers," *Risk Analysis*, Vol. 21, No. 5, 2001, pp. 923–937.

Presidential Policy Directive 21, *Critical Infrastructure Security and Resilience*, Washington, D.C.: The White House, February 12, 2014.

Presidential Policy Directive 40, *National Continuity Policy*, Washington, D.C.: The White House, July 15, 2016.

Public Law 107-296, Homeland Security Act of 2002, November 25, 2002.

Public Law 110-53, Implementing Recommendations of the 9/11 Commission Act of 2007, August 3, 2007.

Slovic, Paul, Baruch Fischhoff, and Sarah Lichtenstein, "Characterizing Perceived Risk," in R. W. Kates, C. Hohenemser, and J. X. Kasperson, eds., *Perilous Progress: Managing the Hazards of Technology*, Boulder, Colo.: Westview Press, 1985, pp. 91–125.

U.S. Department of Homeland Security, "Flows Study," unpublished document provided to RAND, no date.

———, *2010 Quadrennial Homeland Security Review*, Washington, D.C., 2010. As of November 21, 2017:
https://www.dhs.gov/publication/2010-quadrennial-homeland-security-review-qhsr

———, "DHS Policy After Action Report on HSNRC Analysis," unpublished briefing provided to RAND by the DHS Office of Policy, 2012.

———, "2014 Homeland Security National Risk Characterization," unpublished briefing provided to RAND by the DHS Office of Policy, 2014a.

———, *2014 Quadrennial Homeland Security Review*, Washington, D.C., 2014b. As of November 21, 2017:
https://www.dhs.gov/publication/2014-quadrennial-homeland-security-review-qhsr

———, "DHS Mission Statement," 2017. As of November 21, 2017:
https://www.dhs.gov/our-mission

U.S. Department of Homeland Security, Office of Policy, 2011 Strategic National Risk Assessment documentation files, unpublished files provided to RAND, no date.

U.S. Governmental Accountability Office, *Quadrennial Homeland Security Review: Improved Risk Analysis and Stakeholder Consultation Could Enhance Future Reviews*, Washington, D.C., GAO-16-371, March 2016.

Willis, H. H., M. L. DeKay, M. G. Morgan, H. K. Florig, and P. S. Fischbeck, "Ecological Risk Ranking: Development and Evaluation of a Method for Improving Public Participation in Environmental Decision Making," *Risk Analysis*, Vol. 24, 2004, pp. 363–378.

Willis, H. H., J. MacDonald, R. Shih, S. Geschwind, S. Olmstead, J. Hu, A. E. Curtright, G. Cecchine, and M. Moore, "Prioritizing Environmental Health Risks in the UAE," *Risk Analysis*, Vol. 20, No. 12, 2010, pp. 1842–1856.